FIBONACCI SEQUENCE

PI

MATH

for Curious Kids

An illustrated introduction to numbers,
geometry, computing, and more!

SHAPES

DATA

ARCTURUS

ARCTURUS

This edition published in 2022 by Arcturus Publishing Limited
26/27 Bickels Yard, 151–153 Bermondsey Street,
London SE1 3HA

Author: Lynn Huggins-Cooper
Illustrator: Alex Foster
Consultant: Anne Rooney
Designer: Mark Golden
Packaged by Cloud King Creative

ISBN: 978-1-3988-0273-5
CH008272US
Supplier 29, Date 0822, PI 00001703

Printed in China

What is STEM?

STEM is a world-wide initiative that aims to cultivate an interest in Science, Technology, Engineering, and Mathematics, in an effort to promote these disciplines to as wide a variety of students as possible.

CONTENTS

MAGNIFICENT MATHEMATICS

When you tell the time, cook, figure out change, measure things, read timetables, and more—you are using mathematics! Mathematics is used to build theme parks, in medicine, in sports, business, and space travel. Mathematics is everywhere!

We use mathematics to help us figure out money, such as how much things cost and how much change we can expect to be given when we buy things. It can also help us to work out how much more money we need when we are saving money to buy something.

We use mathematics when we measure things, such as ingredients for a recipe.

 ## WHAT IS MATHEMATICS?

Mathematics is the science that deals with shape, quantities, patterns, and arrangements. Mathematics helps us to understand the world around us, and gives us ways to solve problems.

There are lots of different branches of mathematics.
These include:

 # ARITHMETIC

Arithmetic is about numbers. It helps us work out addition, subtraction, division, and multiplication calculations.

1 2 3 4 5
6 7 8 9 0

X = -
÷ +

 # ALGEBRA

Algebra allows us to use unknown quantities (often given letters) with numbers to create a formula, so we can solve problems.

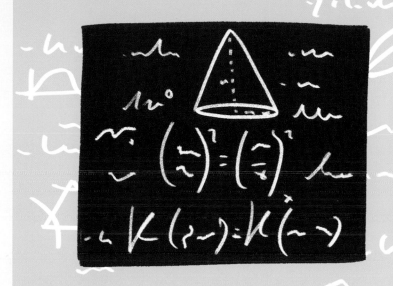

 # GEOMETRY

Geometry is the study of shapes and their properties (such as faces, vertices, and edges).

 # TRIGONOMETRY

Trigonometry is the study of the relationships between the angles and sides of triangles.

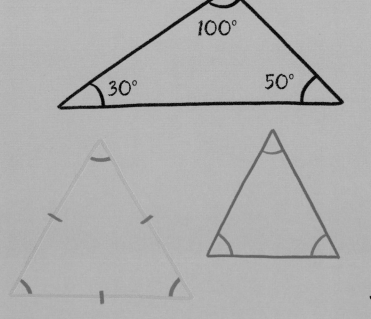

5

CHAPTER 1

NUMBERS

123

People have probably always counted things—
even before they had "numbers."

TALLY STICKS

Archaeologists have found evidence of marks made on bone and stone that suggest people were counting even in prehistoric times. These are called tally sticks.

This stick is called the Lebombo bone. It was found in a cave near the border between South Africa and Eswatini. It is between 44,200 and 43,000 years old. It has 29 markings along one edge. It has been suggested the marks follow the cycle of the moon.

ROMAN NUMERALS

Roman numerals are the numbers that were used by the Roman Empire. Letters were used to represent the value of numbers.

When a symbol appears after a higher value symbol, the number is added. So 23 would be XXIII (20 + 3).

1	2	3	4	5	6	7	8	9
I	II	III	IV	V	VI	VII	VIII	IX

10	20	30	40	50	60	70	80	90
X	XX	XXX	XL	L	LX	LXX	LXXX	XC

When a symbol appears before a higher value symbol, the number is taken away. So 14 would be XIV (10+ "I before 5").

100	200	300	400	500	600	700	800	900
C	CC	CC	CD	D	DC	DCC	DCCC	CM

ACROSS THE WORLD

Roman numerals were used in many parts of the world in the Roman era, because their empire covered much of Europe. Wherever the conquering armies went, they took their system of numbers with them.

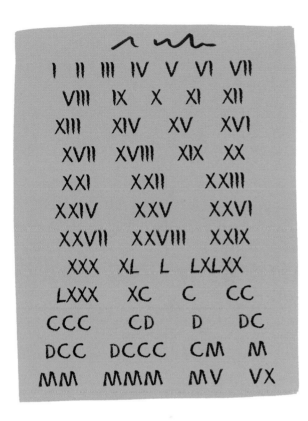

I	II	III	IV	V	VI	VII
VIII	IX	X	XI	XII		
XIII	XIV	XV	XVI			
XVII	XVIII	XIX	XX			
XXI	XXII	XXIII				
XXIV	XXV	XXVI				
XXVII	XXVIII	XXIX				
XXX	XL	L	LXLXX			
LXXX	XC	C	CC			
CCC	CD	D	DC			
DCC	DCCC	CM	M			
MM	MMM	MV	VX			

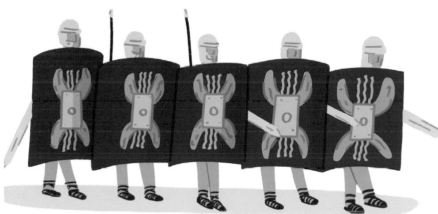

ROMAN NUMERALS TODAY

We still see Roman numerals on some clocks today. For instance, take a look at Big Ben in the Clock Tower of the Palace of Westminster in London.

INDO-ARABIC NUMERALS

Indo-Arabic numbers are the numbers used across much of the world today. They originated in India by the 6th or 7th century. They spread to the west in the work of Middle Eastern scholars such as the mathematician Al-Khwarizmi.

Zero means "no amount."

When you take 0 away from a number, nothing happens—the value is not affected.

$$7 - 0 = 7$$

In the same way, when you add 0 to a number, nothing happens—the value is not affected.

$$7 + 0 = 7$$

Each zero added after a digit increases the value ten-fold.

1 (add a zero as place holder) becomes 10

10 (add a zero as place holder) becomes 100

100 (add a zero as place holder) becomes 1,000

Zero is also used as a place holder in place value systems, such as the decimal system.

1
10
100
1,000

ZERO IN THE ANCIENT WORLD

The ancient Egyptians, Romans, and Greeks had no symbol for zero. Ancient Americans did use a symbol for zero, however. The Olmec people flourished in the area now known as Mexico until around 400 BCE. They had a symbol for zero, which was used as a place holder.

MAYAN AND INCAN ZERO

After the Olmecs, the Mayan civilization also used a symbol for zero. It looked like a turtle shell!

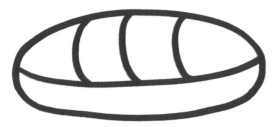

The Incas, who lived in the area now known as Peru, had a form of zero. They used a knotted device called a quipu for counting. The knots stood for different values. The absence of a knot in a particular position stood for zero.

ZERO IN THE MIDDLE AGES

In 825 CE, the Persian mathematician Al-Khwarizmi published a book which combined ancient Greek and Indian mathematics. This book included an explanation of the use of zero. He also said that if no number appears in the place of tens in a calculation, a circle should be used to "keep the rows"—using zero as a place holder. The circle was called sifr.

ZERO IN EUROPE

In 1202, the idea of zero came to Europe (along with the rest of the Indo-Arabic number system) largely through the work of the Italian mathematician Fibonacci. He had studied with the Moors, or Spanish Muslims. That is why the numerals in this number system, still in use today, were known as "Arabic numerals." Fibonacci helped introduce ideas about zero to the study of mathematics in Europe.

UNITY

In mathematics, unity means "one." It is our unit of counting, and the first whole number in the positive number sequence.

OUT OF CURIOSITY

The number 1 has several names. Apart from unity, it is also called "unit" and "identity."

1 SIMPLE!

Any number multiplied by 1 remains unchanged.

$3 \times 1 = 3$

$25 \times 1 = 25$

$168 \times 1 = 168$

$1,265 \times 1 = 1,265$

1 NO CHANGE

You can multiply 1 by itself any number of times and it is always still 1.

$1 \times 1 = 1$

Even when 1 is squared or cubed, it stays the same.

$1^2 = 1$

$1^3 = 1$

So unity squared is the same value as unity, and unity cubed is the same value as unity.

1 POSITIVELY ODD . . .

Unity is the first positive odd number. It is the first and smallest positive integer (a whole number that can be positive, negative, or zero). It is the unit of counting.

The number 1 can do a kind of mathematical magic, too—adding it to any number can change an odd number into an even number and an even number into an odd number!

1 WHERE DID 1 COME FROM?

The modern number 1 used around the world traces its beginnings back to ancient India. In the Brahmi script, 1 was just a line:

1 THE ORIGIN OF 1

A single stroke was used to mark "one" for a long time before the Indo-Arabic numeral 1 was introduced to Europe.

Do you remember the tally sticks on page 6? Each mark there stood for one event or thing being recorded. The strokes were not numerals but each stroke represented one "thing" as it was counted, such as the passing of a day.

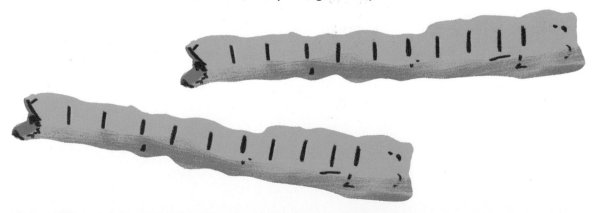

EVEN NUMBERS

Even numbers are numbers that can be divided exactly by 2, with no remainder.

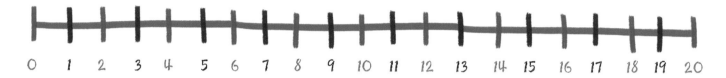

0 2 4 6 8

 ## NUMBER LINES

If you count along in 2s on a number line, starting at zero, you will see a series of even numbers. If you wrote this series down, you would be able to see a pattern.

0 1 2 3 4 5 6 7 8 9 10 11 12 13 14 15 16 17 18 19 20

Can you see the pattern when you look at this number line? The pattern of even numbers is that they always end in 0 2 4 6 8—no matter how large the value!

So, these numbers are all even:

2

16

96

112

678

1,132

11,678

0
2
4

6

8

You can see the pattern straight away, without having to do any calculations. If a number ends in 0, 2, 4, 6, or 8 it is an even number. You can also test the numbers to see if they are even by dividing them by 2. If they divide exactly with no remainder, they are even numbers.

SHARING EVEN NUMBERS

Even numbers of things are easy to share between two people. If you have an even number of grapes or cookies, you can share them exactly with a friend without having to break any in half. Remember, even numbers can always be divided exactly by 2.

TRY IT YOURSELF

Which of these numbers do you think are even?

345   766   821

654   5,432   328

OUT OF CURIOSITY

When we add, subtract, or multiply even numbers the results are always predictable:

even + even = even

even x even = even

even – even = even

Negative numbers (see page 24), such as -2 and -4, can be even, too!

ODD NUMBERS

Odd numbers are numbers that cannot be divided exactly by 2. When odd numbers are divided by 2, they always leave a remainder of 1.

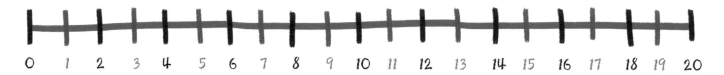

NUMBER LINES

If you count along in 2s on a number line, starting at 1, you will see a series of odd numbers. If you wrote this series down, you would be able to see a pattern.

0 1 2 3 4 5 6 7 8 9 10 11 12 13 14 15 16 17 18 19 20

Can you see the pattern when you look at this number line? The pattern of odd numbers is that they always end in 1 3 5 7 9—no matter how large the value of the number.

So, these numbers are all odd:

5

47

169

2,135

6,121

10,893

You can see the pattern straight away, without having to do any calculations. If the number ends in 1, 3, 5, 7, or 9 it is an odd number. You can test the numbers to see if they are odd by dividing them by 2. If there is a remainder of 1, it's an odd number.

OUT OF CURIOSITY

The sum of 2 odd numbers is always even—try it out by adding odd numbers together and see what you find!

 ODD TIMES

The **product** of two or more odd numbers is always odd. Try it out!

$$3 \text{ (odd)} \times 5 \text{ (odd)} \quad 15 \text{ (odd)}$$

$$9 \text{ (odd)} \times 7 \text{ (odd)} \quad 63 \text{ (odd)}$$

3 x 5 = 15

PRIME NUMBERS

Prime numbers are numbers greater than 1 that can only be divided exactly by themselves and 1. They cannot be divided by any other numbers without leaving a remainder. 19 is an example of a prime number. It can only be divided by 1 and 19. If you divide by any other number there will be a remainder.

11 is a prime number because it cannot be divided exactly by any numbers except 11 and 1.

12 is NOT a prime number because it can be divided exactly by 12, 1, 2, 3, 4, and 6.

1	2	3	4	5	6	7	8	9	10
11	12	13	14	15	16	17	18	19	20
21	22	23	24	25	26	27	28	29	30

FIRST 10 PRIME NUMBERS

There are 10 prime numbers under 30. They are:

2, 3, 5, 7, 11, 13, 17, 19, 23, 29

None of these numbers can be divided exactly by anything but themselves and 1. 2 is the only even prime number.

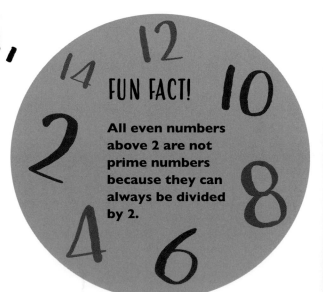

FUN FACT!

All even numbers above 2 are not prime numbers because they can always be divided by 2.

PRIME NUMBERS IN THE REAL WORLD

Prime numbers are used in cyber security—making the information we share over the Internet safer. Software engineers use prime numbers to **encrypt** (make hard to read and decipher) things that need to be kept secure, such as credit card details, messaging programs such as WhatsApp, and medical records. Almost every online purchase uses prime numbers to keep the transaction secure.

Software engineers use huge prime numbers and multiply them together to make really large numbers with original **factors** (the two original prime numbers) to encrypt information. Information is kept secure because it would take years to work out which original factors were used.

 # PRIME NUMBERS TO 100

These numbers are the prime numbers up to 100. Can you explain why?

OUT OF CURIOSITY

The world's largest known prime number is nearly 25 million digits long!

2	3	5	7	11	13
17	19	23	29	31	37
41	43	47	53	59	61
67	71	73	83	89	97

FACTORS

A factor is a number that divides into another number exactly, with no remainder. 1 and the number itself are always factors of any given number.

POSITIVE FACTORS OF 10:

1, 2, 5, and 10

FACTORS OF 100:

1, 2, 4, 5, 10, 20, 25, 50, and 100

 ## FINDING FACTORS

To find factors of a number, start by looking to see if it is an even number. If it is, you know 2 is a factor. Then see if the number ends in zero. If it does, 10 is a factor. Factors are whole numbers—not fractions of numbers.

FACTOR PAIRS

Factor pairs are combinations of two factors that, when multiplied together, equal a given number. The factor pairs of 100 are:

POSITIVE FACTORS:

$$1 \times 100 = 100$$

$$2 \times 50 = 100$$

$$4 \times 25 = 100$$

$$5 \times 20 = 100$$

$$10 \times 10 = 100$$

$$20 \times 5 = 100$$

$$25 \times 4 = 100$$

$$50 \times 2 = 100$$

$$100 \times 1 = 100$$

FACTORING

Factoring is the process of breaking numbers down into all of their factors (the numbers that can divide into the number exactly). Take a number and factorize it.

LEARN YOUR TIMES TABLES

Your times tables are really useful for helping you to work out the factors of numbers.

You know that 3 x 7 = 21, so you know that 3 and 7 are both factors of 21.

FRACTIONS AND DECIMALS

A fraction is a part of a whole. Think about what happens when you slice a pizza into parts. If those parts are equal, they can tell us about fractions.

   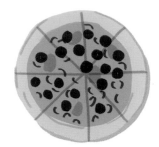

 ## NUMERATOR AND DENOMINATOR

Fractions have a numerator and a denominator. The numerator is the number on the top of a fraction. The denominator is the number on the bottom. The numerator gives us information about how many parts of the "whole" we have. The denominator tells us how many parts the "whole" was divided into.

$$\frac{\text{NUMERATOR}}{\text{DENOMINATOR}}$$

¼ means 1 part of a whole that has been divided into 4 parts.

⅞ means 7 parts of a whole that has been divided into 8 parts.

 ## PROPER FRACTIONS

A "proper fraction" is a fraction where the numerator is less than the denominator. Proper fractions are always less than 1 whole.

$\frac{1}{2}$ = 1 part of a whole cut into 2 parts

$\frac{9}{10}$ = 9 part of a whole cut into 10 parts

$\frac{3}{4}$ = 3 part of a whole cut into 4 parts

IMPROPER FRACTIONS

Improper fractions are fractions where the numerator is larger than the denominator. Improper fractions are greater than 1 whole. They are "top heavy."

$\frac{3}{2}$ = 3 parts of a whole divided into 2 parts = 3 halves = $1\frac{1}{2}$

$\frac{5}{4}$ = 5 parts of a whole divided into 4 parts = 5 quarters = $1\frac{1}{4}$

$\frac{8}{3}$ = 8 parts of a whole divided into 3 parts = 8 thirds = $2\frac{2}{3}$

 # MIXED FRACTIONS

Mixed fractions have both a "whole number" and a fraction of a whole number. Here are some examples of mixed fractions:

$1\frac{1}{2}$

$8\frac{3}{4}$

$4\frac{5}{6}$

WHAT ARE DECIMALS?

When decimal points are used in numbers, the number to the right of the decimal point is a kind of fraction.

1.1 is the same as $1\frac{1}{10}$

1.01 is the same as 1 and $\frac{1}{100}$

1.001 is the same as $1\frac{1}{1000}$

 # WHAT IS THE RELATIONSHIP BETWEEN FRACTIONS AND DECIMALS?

Fractions and decimals can give us the same information:

0.25 is the same as $\frac{1}{4}$ 0.5   is the same as $\frac{1}{2}$

0.3   is the same as $\frac{3}{10}$ 0.75 is the same as $\frac{3}{4}$

We can change fractions into decimal equivalents by seeing the line that divides the numerator from the denominator as a division sign ÷. To convert a fraction to a decimal, we divide the numerator by the denominator.

$\frac{1}{2}$ is the same as $1 \div 2 = 0.5$

INFINITY

Infinity means "without end." We say that things are infinite
when they go on forever, like space or numbers.

Infinity means an endless number of the things being described. Infinity is not a real number;
It is an idea. It is something that never ends. It cannot be measured.

∞ INFINITY AND THE ANCIENT WORLD

The ancient Greeks called infinity apeiron. It meant boundless and formless. One of the
earliest discussions of infinity in mathematics was about the **ratio** between the diagonal and
side of a square. Aristotle (384–322 BCE) rejected "actual" infinity, but he did recognize the
potential infinity of being able to count and never stop counting.

∞ BOUNDLESS SPACE

It's not just numbers that are infinite! Space might be infinite if it carries on forever. We don't know if space has an end and often call it "infinite."

∞ SYMBOL FOR INFINITY

We can use a symbol to stand for infinity. It looks like an 8 lying on its side and was created by the mathematician John Wallis in 1665.

∞ ENDLESS NUMBERS

You could count forever—numbers have no end as you could always add another one. Mathematicians call the endlessness of numbers "infinity."

10
20 30 40
50 60 70 80
90 100 110 120 130
140 150 160 170 180 190
200 210 220 230 240 250
260 270 280 290 300 310
320 330 340 350 360 370

∞ ON AND ON

Even a computer couldn't count to infinity. If we could have set a computer counting one number a second at the time of the dinosaurs it would still be going and continue forever!

NEGATIVE NUMBERS

A negative number is a real number that is less than zero. When you count backward from zero, you start counting in negative numbers. The numbers that are more than zero are called positive numbers. Zero is neither negative nor positive.

NUMBERS TO THE RIGHT OF 0 (ZERO) ARE POSITIVE

-10 -9 -8 -7 -6 -5 -4 -3 -2 -1 0 1 2 3 4 5 6 7 8 9 10

NUMBERS TO THE LEFT OF 0 (ZERO) ARE NEGATIVE

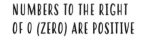 NEGATIVE NUMBERS IN HISTORY

The use of negative numbers dates from the Chinese Han Dynasty (202 BCE–220 CE). In the 7th century, the Indian scholar Brahmagupta wrote about the use of negative numbers.

Islamic mathematicians continued working on negative numbers and developed rules about the way they behaved. For instance, negative numbers were used in early accounting, where debts were recorded as negative amounts of money.

NEGATIVE NUMBERS IN SCIENCE

Science uses negative numbers in lots of ways.

TEMPERATURE COLDER THAN ZERO

Negative numbers can be used for measurements on a scale that can go below zero. One example is temperature. The Celsius scale sets zero degrees as the freezing point of water, but temperatures can go much lower than that. In Antarctica, it can reach nearly -148°F (-100°C)!

In geography, negative numbers are used to show the measurements of the Earth's surface when it falls below sea level.

NEGATIVE NUMBERS IN EVERYDAY LIFE

You can see negative numbers everywhere if you look closely!

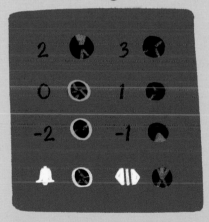

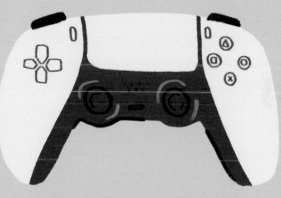

The buttons in elevators use negative numbers to show floors below ground, such as the basement.

In video games, negative numbers are used to show damage, loss of "lives," or using up of a resource.

When playing an audio file, negative numbers are sometimes used to show the time left to play.

CHAPTER 2

AMAZING NUMBERS

$3 \times 6 = 18$

Some numbers are special. Some create patterns, such as the **Fibonacci sequence**, that are found in nature—in shells and plants, for example, creating beautiful curved lines. Patterns can be found everywhere in nature. These sequences and patterns have been identified and discussed by great thinkers and mathematicians, such as Pythagoras and Descartes, for centuries.

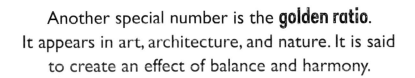

Another special number is the **golden ratio**. It appears in art, architecture, and nature. It is said to create an effect of balance and harmony.

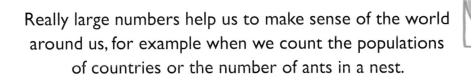

Really large numbers help us to make sense of the world around us, for example when we count the populations of countries or the number of ants in a nest.

Fractals are geometric patterns that repeat with different sizes and scales in the same object. Fractals often appear in nature: in snowflakes, ferns, and forked lightning, for example.

THE FIBONACCI SEQUENCE

The Fibonacci sequence is a series of numbers. The next number in the sequence is found by adding the two numbers before it—it's simple!

$$0 + 1 = 1 \qquad 1 + 1 = 2 \qquad 1 + 2 = 3 \qquad 2 + 3 = 5$$

And so on!

$$0, 1, 1, 2, 3, 5, 8, 13, 21, 34 \ldots$$

We call it the Fibonacci sequence because it was made famous in Europe by a man named Leonardo Pisano Bigollo, known as Fibonacci. He wrote a book in 1202 called *Liber Abaci*. He helped to spread the use of Indo-Arabic numerals that most parts of the world use today:

$$1, 2, 3, 4, 5, 6, 7, 8, 9, 10$$

Before that, many people used Roman numerals:

$$I, II, III, IV, V, VI, VII, VIII, IX, X$$

Fibonacci did not discover the sequence, even though he made it famous. It was already known in India in the work of mathematician Virahanka, who lived some time between the 6th and 8th century.

LADDER OF LIFE

The Fibonacci spiral is found in lots of places in nature. The number of petals on a flower, seeds on a seed head or inside a fruit, spikes on pine cones, and leaves on a stem are all examples of Fibonacci numbers—look around you! If you count the petals on a flower you are likely to find a Fibonacci number.

The Fibonacci sequence is sometimes called "Nature's Code."

OUT OF CURIOSITY

Cut an apple in half across the core and you will see a star with 5 points made from seeds: a Fibonacci number.

DID YOU KNOW?

In the US, November 23rd is Fibonacci Day! That is because it has the digits 1, 1, 2, 3.

1,1 because November is the eleventh month and 2,3 because it is the 23rd day.

GOLDEN RATIO

The golden ratio is a special number just about equal to 1.618. The ratio of 1.618 to 1 is said to create a beautiful shape in art, architecture—and even in human beauty!

FACES AND THE GOLDEN RATIO

The human face is seen as "attractive" when all of the features like eyes, nose, and mouth are symmetrical, and the ratio of the length to the width of the face is 1.6 to 1. That means for a face to been seen as beautiful that the length is roughly 1½ times the width—amazing!

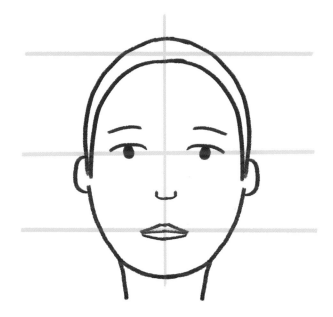

SYMBOL

The golden ratio may be expressed using the Greek letter phi.

Some mathematicians say that the Parthenon, an ancient Greek temple completed in around 438 BCE, has proportions that match the golden ratio. The width of its front facade is roughly 1.6 times its height, making it look elegant.

THE GOLDEN RATIO IN ART

Many artists have used the golden ratio in their work as it is pleasing to the human eye. Leonardo da Vinci called it the "divine proportion" and used it in many works, including the *Mona Lisa*.

THE GOLDEN RATIO AND THE FIBONACCI SEQUENCE

Interestingly, there is a relationship between the golden ratio and Fibonacci sequence. After the first few numbers in the sequence, the ratio between each number and the next approaches the golden ratio.

THE GOLDEN RATIO IN NATURE

Draw a rectangle with sides in the ratio 1:1.618. Use the longer side as the shorter side of another rectangle of the same proportions drawn around the first, then keep going. Draw a spiral through the opposite corners of the squares in the set you have drawn.

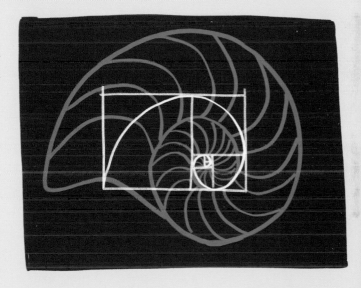

When we make squares with Fibonacci numbers, they create a spiral that is seen in many shapes in nature, including snails' shells.

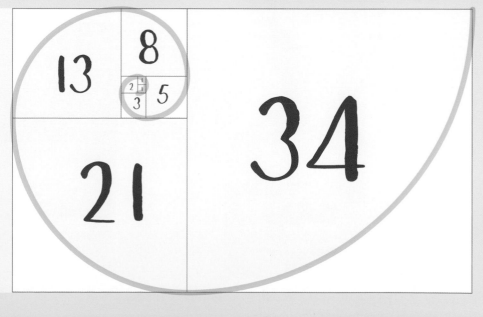

❄ FRACTALS ❄

Fractals are patterns that repeat at different scales. They are not at all random, but are a single geometric pattern repeated at different magnifications— so they are a useful part of everyday life in a variety of settings.

❄ FRACTALS IN NATURE

Leaves and snowflakes contain fractals. So does Romanesco cauliflower and pineapples!

❄ FRACTALS IN MEDICINE

Fractals are used in medicine. Doctors use fractal patterns in blood vessels to learn about some types of illness.

❄ FRACTALS AT HOME

TV antennae harness the power of fractals to work with a range of **frequencies**—and that allows us to watch TV!

FRACTAL SHAPES IN MATHEMATICS

Fractal shapes created by mathematicians include the Koch curve (below), Koch snowflake (below right), and the Sierpinski triangle (left). The Koch snowflake was one of the first fractals to be described.

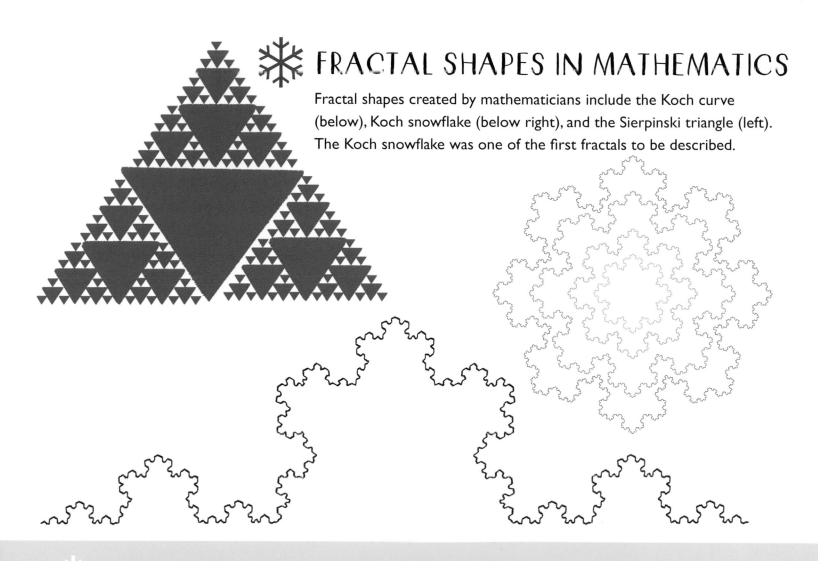

FRACTALS IN MATHEMATICS

The mathematician Benoit Mandelbrot (1924–2010) first studied and named fractals. He looked at shapes in nature and said that things that were usually seen to be "rough" or "chaotic" like shorelines and clouds actually had a type of order. He created a formula to explain it. Mandelbrot was the first person to use computers (he had access to the computers at IBM) to make fractal images.

A famous fractal pattern is named after him, called the Mandelbrot set. The pattern is infinite, repeating at a smaller and smaller scale.

ANIMALS AND NUMBER SENSE

Did you know that some animals have a sense of number? Amazing though it is, research has shown that some animals, such as primates, birds, and even fish, have an idea of "how many." They are not counting in the sense that you might count, but they have an idea of what mathematicians call numerosity. That means an estimation of the amount of things rather than exact "counting." Animals have been shown to notice when one of a litter of young is missing, for example.

 ## CLEVER HANS

In the early 20th century, a man named Wilhelm von Osten claimed his horse Clever Hans could count. He showed the horse carrying out mathematical **operations** when asked questions—or even given written questions! Sadly, an investigation by Oskar Pfungst found that Clever Hans was not "doing mathematics" but was responding to the body language of the people asking the questions. Still a very clever horse though!

JACOB THE RAVEN

Otto Koehler carried out research on number sense in animals from the 1920s to the 1970s. One of his subjects was a raven named Jacob. This clever bird was able to reliably count up to 5 objects.

 ## LEVER ACTION!

In the 1980s and 1990s, several research projects, including the work of Francis Mechner, John Platt, and David Johnson, found that both rats and pigeons were able to press a lever more than a given number of times in order to release food.

 ## CAN ANTS CALCULATE?

Red wood ants are very social. They live in colonies and communicate with each other frequently about food, directions, and threats. In an experiment, scouts seemed to count up to 20 in a "counting maze," telling foragers where to go to find food. The ants seemed to use simple additions and subtractions to give their instructions.

ooo LARGE NUMBERS ooo

Really large numbers can be hard to really understand. It can be confusing when numbers have a whole string of zeros. In order to get a clear picture in your head, it helps if you think about everyday things, and what a million or perhaps billion of them would look like.

ooo MILLIONS

A million is written as 1 followed by 6 zeros.

1,000,000

It can be easier to understand if you think of how the value relates to a number you understand. A million is "worth" 1,000 lots of 1,000.

1,000 lots of 1,000 = 1 million

1,000 x 1,000 = 1,000,000

ooo WHAT IS COUNTED IN MILLIONS?

Populations of cities and countries are counted in millions. The world's biggest city is Tokyo in Japan, with around 38 million people living there.
Find out how many million people live in your country.

OUT OF CURIOSITY

There are 1 million seconds in 11.5 days and 1 million minutes in around 2 years.

000 BILLIONS

A billion is the equivalent of a thousand million. It is written as the numeral 1 followed by 9 zeros.

1,000,000,000

1,000 lots of 1,000,000 = 1 billion

1,000 × 1,000,000 = 1,000,000,000

000 WHAT IS COUNTED IN BILLIONS?

The population of the world is counted in billions. By March 2020, the population of the world stood at around 7,800,000,000.

OUT OF CURIOSITY

If you counted non-stop, one number per second, it would take you nearly 32 years to count up to 1 billion!

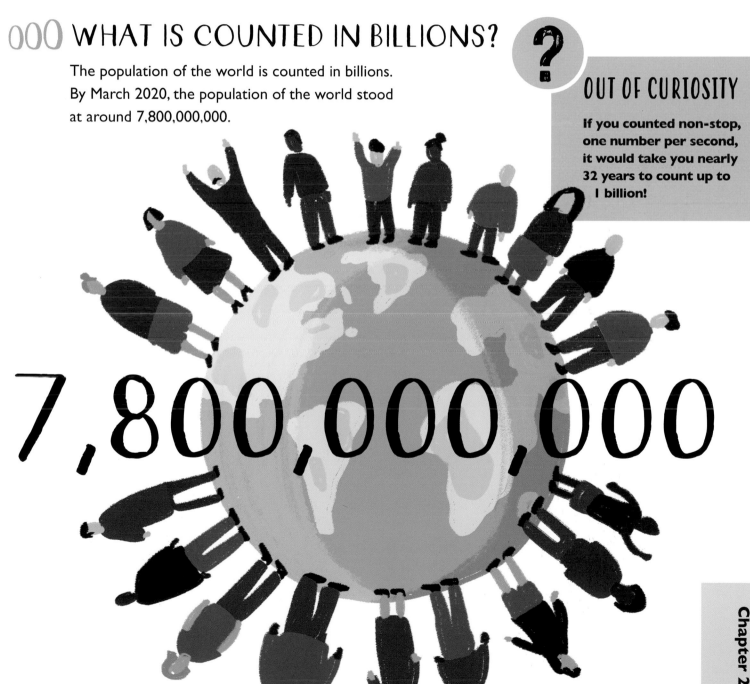

7,800,000,000

HUGE NUMBERS

Some numbers have such large values that they are not used often outside of mathematics or astronomy.

We have:

Trillion (twelve zeros) ● ● ● ● ● ● ● ● ● ● ● ●
1,000,000,000,000

Quadrillion (fifteen zeros) ● ● ● ● ● ● ● ● ● ● ● ● ● ● ●
1,000,000,000,000,000

Quintillion (eighteen zeros) ● ● ● ● ● ● ● ● ● ● ● ● ● ● ● ● ● ●
1,000,000,000,000,000,000

Sextillion (twenty-one zeros) ●
1,000,000,000,000,000,000,000

Septillion (twenty-four zeros) ●
1,000,000,000,000,000,000,000,000

Octillion (twenty-seven zeros) ●
1,000,000,000,000,000,000,000,000,000

Nonillion (thirty zeros) ●
1,000,000,000,000,000,000,000,000,000,000

Decillion (thirty-three zeros) ●
1,000,000,000,000,000,000,000,000,000,000,000

 # WHAT ARE THEY USED FOR?

Many of these numbers are used for the calculation of mathematical ideas. In everyday life, we do not use them very often. Scientists sometimes use large numbers. When physicists talk about the speed of light, they use trillions, for example. Light travels approximately 5.9 trillion miles (9.5 trillion km) in a year. That distance is called a "light year."

Earth is at least 320 light years from Polaris, the bright North Star.

STARRY, STARRY NIGHT...

Have you ever looked up at the sky on a clear night and seen bright, shining stars filling the sky? Counting them all would be hard! There are between 100 and 300 sextillion stars in the Universe.

DATA

Data is a set of observations collected for a purpose.
There are different kinds of data:

QUALITATIVE DATA

This data describes something.
An example might be opinions such
as the best beaches or least
tasty snacks.

QUANTITATIVE DATA

This data counts something, and gives
numerical information. An example
might be recording the heights of
people in your class.

Quantitative data can be discrete
or continuous.

DISCRETE DATA

This is counted in whole numbers.
It has a **finite** number of possible
values. An example is the days in the week.

CONTINUOUS DATA

This is measured and can have an
infinite number of possible values
within a given range. An example is
the temperature of a place over the
course of a month.

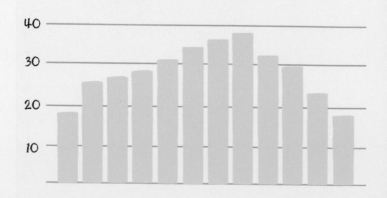

HOW IS DATA COLLECTED?

Data can be collected in lots of ways. It can be collected by observation, such as a traffic survey where passing vehicles are counted.

It can also be collected by a sample or census. A sample is where data is collected from a group; a census is where a whole population is asked for information.

If you had a group of 1,000 children who attended a school and asked every member of the group which pet they owned (if any) that would be an example of a census. If you asked just one class, that would be a sample. Samples give less accurate data than a census but are easier to organize.

WHY IS DATA COLLECTION IMPORTANT?

It is important to collect data to help people decide what action to take. Governments collect data, for example, to help them decide on policies about education, health, and employment. Data collected in a census tells them how many children will need to start school in 5 years so they can plan school places.

DATA HANDLING AND STATISTICS

Once data has been collected, it is processed to find the information worth sharing. Information such as statistics can help people to make decisions.

WHAT ARE STATISTICS?

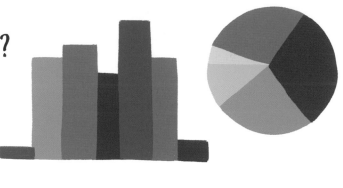

Statistics is the science of data. It collects, analyzes, and presents data. Statistics can be used to help study and predict things, such as weather patterns. They are used in medicine, economics (how money and goods change hands), and marketing (selling things). A person who works with statistics is called a statistician. Data can be displayed in different ways, such as **graphs**. Displays help people to make sense of statistics.

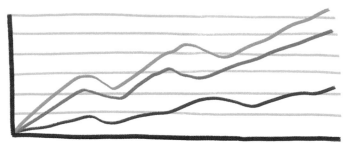

PROBABILITY

Doctors use statistics to help them understand how diseases spread. Statistics can help to predict how many people in a population will probably catch flu over the winter, for example. This helps doctors to predict how many doses of vaccine they will need and how many sick people may need to visit the doctor. Engineers also use statistics to work out the **probability** of projects finishing on time.

WEATHER FORECASTS

Have you ever watched a weather forecast on TV? Statistics are important in predicting weather patterns. Powerful computers use statistics functions to compare weather conditions with previous patterns to predict what will happen.

STATISTICS IN POLITICS

Politicians use statistics in campaigns to help them to know their chance of winning an election. News channels also use statistics to help to predict the results.

STATISTICS IN INSURANCE

People pay for insurance so that, if things go wrong, they have financial help. Car insurance pays for car repairs after an accident. Home insurance pays for damage due to fire or floods, for example. The money paid for insurance is called a premium. It is calculated by working out the risk of something bad happening, and the cost to the insurance company of paying for repairs.

STATISTICS EVERYWHERE!

Statistics are also used in business, sport, education, finance, research, and government. It is impossible to live modern life without statistics playing their part!

PRODUCTS AND FACTORS

In mathematics, a product is the value found by multiplying two or more numbers together.

$$3 \times 6 = 18$$

18 is the product of 3 and 6

$$5 \times 4 = 20$$

20 is the product of 5 and 4

⧗ KEEP IT POSITIVE!

The product of two positive numbers is always positive. That doesn't seem too surprising. However, the product of two negative numbers is also positive.

$$-4 \times -5 = 20$$

FACTORS

A factor is the mathematical opposite of a product. A factor is the number you multiply with other factors to get a product.

3 and 6 are factors of 18

A number can have just two factors or many.

 # FACTORING IN EVERYDAY LIFE

You may sometimes think, "When will I ever use this mathematics skill outside the classroom?" The answer is that factoring is used in many places! Factoring is basic mathematics that reverses multiplication to find the numbers that multiply together to make a bigger number.

When you divide something into equal parts, you use factoring. For example, if 6 children grew strawberry plants and the plants gave 24 strawberries, it would be fair to share them out so that each child received 4 strawberries each. Dividing 24 by 6 gives 4, so each child receives 4 strawberries.

Factoring can also be used when exchanging money for smaller coins and notes.

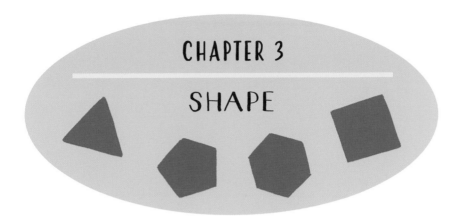

CHAPTER 3

SHAPE

Shapes are everywhere—all around us! Have a look around you. Everything can be broken down into shapes. The mathematics of shape is called geometry.

We talk about shapes in terms of dimensions.
In mathematics, width, length, and height are dimensions.

A line has 1 dimension. It has length but no width.

Then there are 2D shapes such as circles, squares, triangles, and more.
They have length and width. They are flat plane figures and do not have any depth.

There are also 3D shapes such as spheres, cubes, pyramids, and more.
Three-dimensional shapes have three dimensions—length, width, and height.
They are solid figures, and have depth.

POLYGONS AND POLYHEDRONS

Polygons are 2D shapes made up of straight lines, angles, and points. The word polygon is a Greek word meaning "many" and "angle." Any shapes with curved sides are not polygons.

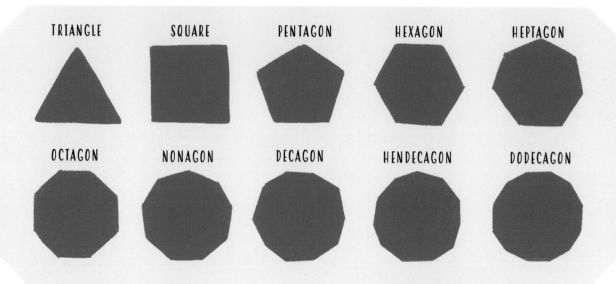

TRIANGLE　　SQUARE　　PENTAGON　　HEXAGON　　HEPTAGON

OCTAGON　　NONAGON　　DECAGON　　HENDECAGON　　DODECAGON

REGULAR POLYGONS

Regular polygons have sides that are all the same length and internal angles (angles inside the shape) that are all the same.

This is a regular heptagon, with seven straight sides.

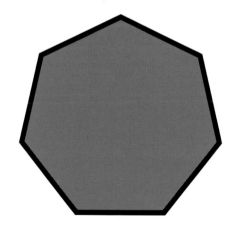

IRREGULAR POLYGONS

Irregular polygons have sides with different lengths and their interior angles may all be different.

This is an irregular heptagon because its sides are not the same length and its interior angles are not the same.

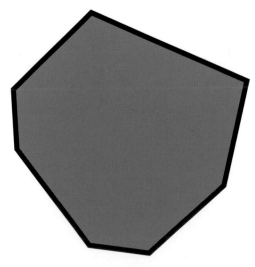

SPOT THE DIFFERENCE

Look at these triangles and **quadrilaterals**. Can you see why some are regular polygons and others are irregular polygons?

 ## POLYGONS IN NATURE

You can see lots of polygons in the world around you. For example, honeycombs have regular polygons called hexagons, with six sides.

You can also see hexagons on snake skin.

POLYHEDRONS

A **polyhedron** is a 3D shape with flat faces and flat edges. The name comes from the Greek *poly* meaning "many" and *hedron* meaning "face." 3D shapes with curved surfaces are not polyhedrons.

A cube and a pyramid are examples of polyhedrons.

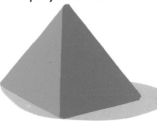

A cone and a sphere are not polyhedrons as they have curved surfaces.

SHAPES WITH CURVES

Some 2D shapes have curved edges, such as circles and **ellipses**. 3D shapes with curved edges include spheres, cylinders, and cones. If you look around you, you can see shapes with curves everywhere!

☾ CIRCLE

Circles are 2D shapes with curved edges. An example is a coin. The shape's edge is always an equal distance from the center. Circles are the most symmetrical shapes in the Universe, with nearly infinite lines of **symmetry**— wherever you draw a line that cuts a circle in two through the center, you will have a reflected image on each side of the line!

ELLIPSE

An ellipse is a 2D shape with curved edges. It has two **axes** running through the center.

The major axis is the long axis and the minor axis is the shorter one. An ellipse has reflection symmetry on either side of its axes.

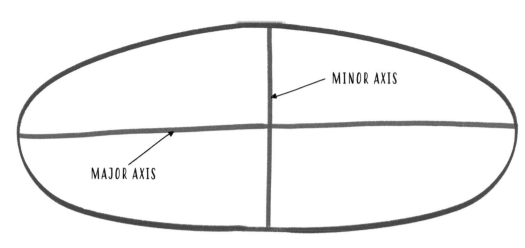

MINOR AXIS

MAJOR AXIS

SPHERE

A sphere is a 3D shape with curved sides. It is perfectly round. A ball is a sphere. Planets are roughly spheres. Every point on the surface of a sphere is an equal distance from its center.

CONE

A cone is a 3D shape—a pyramid with a circle for its base. A tasty example is an ice cream cone! You also find cones on the end of sharp things, like nails used to build things from wood. You may have used some in your shop classes at school!

CYLINDER

A cylinder is a 3D shape with curved edges. A drink can is a cylinder, and so is a wheel. Cylinders are often used for storage because they have a flat bottom so they can be stood upright and even stacked.

If you flattened a cylinder, you would see a rectangle and 2 circles.

CIRCUMFERENCE AND MORE

Circumference is a measure of the distance all the way around the edge, or perimeter, of a circle. An **arc** is a section of the circumference.

Mathematicians talk about a special number called **pi** (see page 54), which is the circumference of a circle divided by its **diameter**.

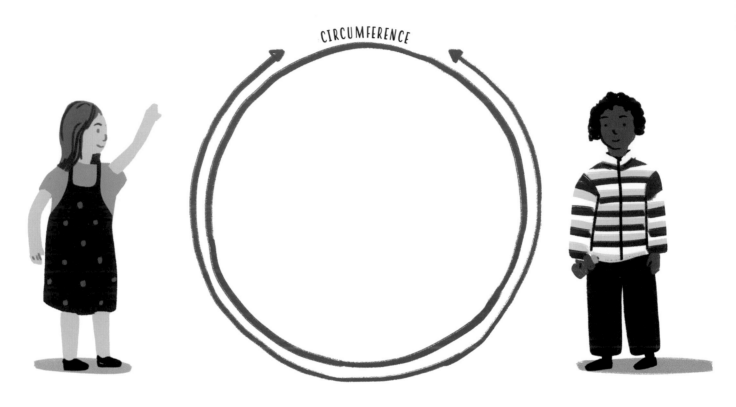

CIRCUMFERENCE

 ## RADIUS

The radius of a circle is the distance between the center of the circle and the edge, or perimeter, of the circle. The radius is half the length of the diameter. Mathematicians use **r** for the length of a circle's radius.

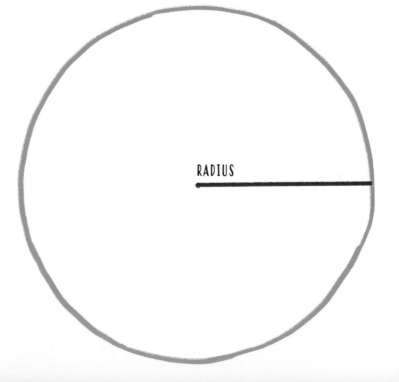

RADIUS

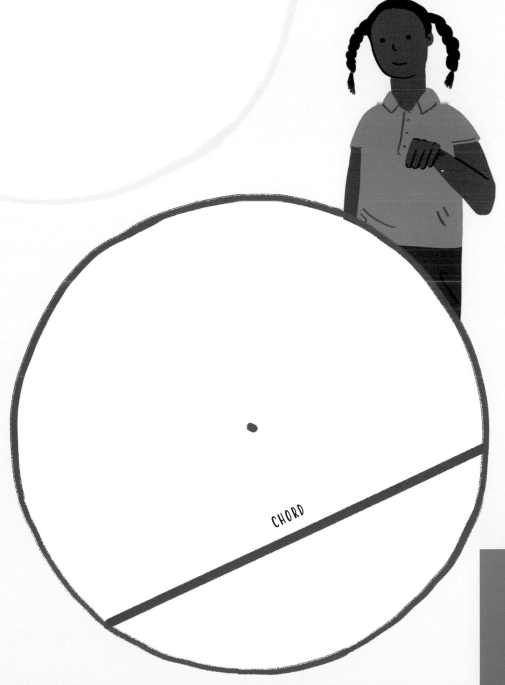

DIAMETER

The diameter of a circle is the distance running across a circle through the center, from edge to edge. The diameter is double the length of the radius.

DIAMETER

CHORD

A chord is a straight line that joins two points on the circumference of a circle. The diameter is a special kind of chord—and it is the longest chord possible, because it goes from one edge of the circle across the center to the other side.

CHORD

Pi is a special number. It can be written using the π symbol, a letter from the Greek alphabet. The letter is the first letter of the Greek word for perimeter. Pi is the ratio of the distance around a circle—the circumference—to its diameter. It doesn't matter how big a circle is, the circumference of any circle is around 3.14 times its diameter—and that "around 3.14" is the value of pi.

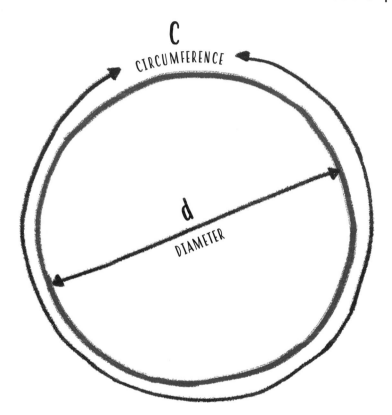

π EQUATION FOR Pi

We can write this rule as an equation that means pi equals circumference divided by diameter.

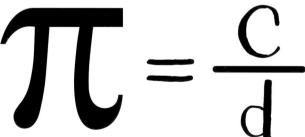

$$\pi = \frac{c}{d}$$

π INFINITE NUMBER

Pi is an infinite number—the numbers after the decimal point keep going on and on. It starts 3.14159265358979323846433 and goes on forever!

3.14159265358979323846...

π THE QUEST FOR Pi

In around 1550 BCE, Egyptian scholar Ahmes gave a rough value for pi in a document called the Rhind Papyrus.

Babylonians discussed pi and explored it by making huge circles and measuring the circumference and diameter with long ropes to help their calculations.

π USING Pi

Pi is used in astronomy to work out **orbits**. It is also used for calculating the area of circles. The area of a circle is pi times the radius squared—$A = \pi r^2$.

π ARCHIMEDES AND ON

The Greek mathematician Archimedes used a 96-sided polygon drawn inside a circle to find the value of pi in 250 BCE. The Greco-Roman scientist Ptolemy gave pi a value equivalent to 3.1416 in around 150 CE. By 500 CE, Chinese scholars including Zu Chongzhi used a 16,384-sided polygon to work out the value with even more accuracy.

π CLOSER AND CLOSER

Persian astronomer Jamshid Al-Kashi produced a value for pi accurate to the equivalent of 16 digits in 1424. By 1621, Dutch scientist Willebrord Snellius calculated to 34 digits. By 1630, Austrian astronomer Christoph Grienberger reached 38 digits. Today, pi can be calculated by **artificial intelligence**—but of course, it is still an infinite number!

QUADRILATERALS AND CUBOIDS

Quadrilaterals are four-sided shapes with straight edges. Quad means "four" and lateral means "sides." All of a quadrilateral's internal angles add up to 360° (see page 60). Quadrilaterals and **cuboids** are important shapes as they are fairly strong and fit together easily, so they are used often in buildings.

 ## PARALLELOGRAM

A parallelogram is a quadrilateral that has two pairs of **parallel** sides. The opposite sides must be an equal length. Parallelograms have four edges and four **vertices** (where edges meet).

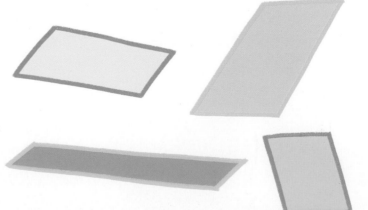

SQUARE

A square is a special kind of parallelogram whose sides and angles are all equal.

A square is a 2D shape with four equal sides. Opposite sides of a square are parallel, and all sides are the same length. Each corner, or vertex, of a square is a right angle, or 90°.

RECTANGLE

A rectangle is a type of parallelogram. It is a 2D shape with two pairs of equal sides.

Like a square, each corner, or vertex, is a right angle, or 90°.

CUBOID

A cuboid is a 3D shape. Most boxes are cuboids. Cuboids have six rectangular faces, and all of their angles are right angles. A cuboid is also a rectangular prism, as it has the same cross-section along its length. That means that, if you cut a slice of a cuboid, you would still see the same shape.

CUBE

A cube is a cuboid with sides that are all the same length. Like all cuboids, cubes have six faces and 12 edges. They have eight vertices, or corners. At each vertex, three edges meet. A cube is a platonic solid. That means that all of its faces are the same regular polygon (or shape) and the same number of polygons meet at each vertex.

TRIANGULAR SHAPES

Triangular shapes are very strong and are used often in architecture and building, just like squares, cubes, and cuboids. We see triangles in roofs in particular, where their strong shape but slanted sides allow rain and snow to run off. That means water will be less likely to damage the roof, so triangles save money, too!

TRIANGLE

A triangle has three straight sides and three vertices. The angles inside a triangle all add up to 180° (see page 60).

There are different types of triangles:

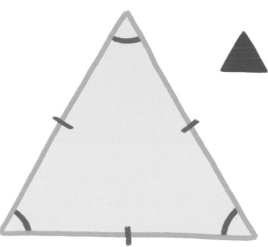

EQUILATERAL TRIANGLE

Equilateral triangles have three equal sides and three equal angles. The angles inside a triangle add up to 180°, so that means each angle is 60°.

ISOSCELES TRIANGLE

Isosceles triangles have two equal sides and two interior (inside) angles, called base angles, that are the same.

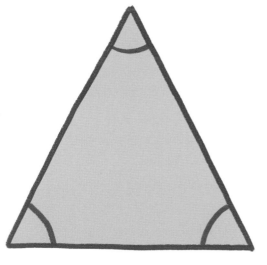

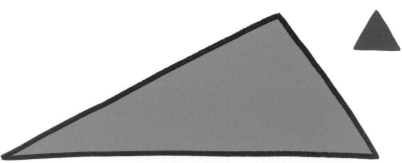

SCALENE TRIANGLE

Scalene triangles have three sides of different lengths and three different interior angles—but the angles still add up to 180°.

RIGHT-ANGLED TRIANGLE

In a right-angled triangle, one of the interior angles is 90°, so the other two angles add up to 90° together—because remember, the angles in a triangle must add up to 180°.

 # PYRAMID

Pyramids are 3D shapes that have four triangular faces. Pyramids can be square or triangular based. A square-based pyramid has five faces and five vertices. It has eight edges.

A triangular-based pyramid has four faces and four vertices. It has six edges.

 ## OUT OF CURIOSITY

A triangular-based pyramid with equal sides is called a tetrahedron.

 # TRIANGULAR PRISM

A triangular prism is a 3D shape. Three sides are parallelograms and the opposite ends of the shape are triangles. Some tents are the shape of triangular prisms!

ANGLES

Angles are made wherever two lines meet. Angles are measured in degrees.
A complete turn (if you held out your arms and turned in a complete circle) is 360°.

PROTRACTORS

Angles can be measured with an instrument called a protractor.
You can get 180° and 360° protractors.

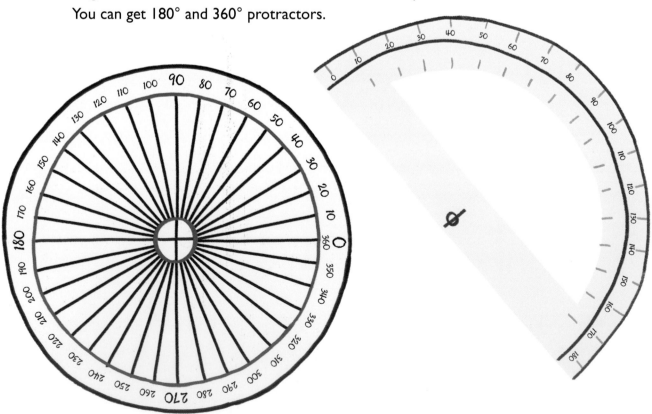

There are different types of angles:

RIGHT ANGLES

A right angle is exactly 90°. Right angles are represented in mathematical diagrams by a square, so you immediately know it is a right angle.

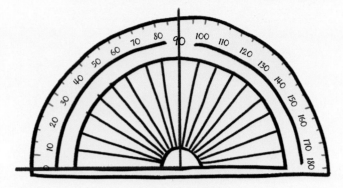

ACUTE ANGLES

Acute angles are angles of less than 90°. They are smaller than right angles.

OBTUSE ANGLES

Obtuse angles are angles of between 90° and 180°.

STRAIGHT ANGLES

A straight angle is exactly 180°.

REFLEX ANGLES

A reflex angle is between 180° and 360°.

When mathematicians draw angles, they draw a curved line inside (unless it is a 90° angle, which is drawn with a square).

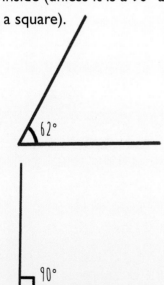

SYMMETRY

When we say a shape has symmetry in mathematics, we mean that one side looks the same as the other. There are different types of symmetry, such as **reflectional** and rotational **symmetry**.

REFLECTIONAL SYMMETRY

Reflectional symmetry is also called line symmetry or mirror symmetry.

If you can draw a line through the axis of a shape and both sides are the same— a reflection of each other— a shape has reflectional symmetry. Butterflies have reflectional symmetry.

You can have fun with a small, straight-edged safety mirror if you look for the mirror symmetry of pictures. Use a mirror to see the other half of these shapes: Put the mirror on the dotted line and see what happens!

◎ MULTIPLE LINES OF SYMMETRY

All regular polygons have at least one line of symmetry. Some shapes have multiple lines of symmetry.

You can explore lines of symmetry in shapes by cutting the shapes out of construction paper. Fold them in half to make the lines of symmetry. You can draw the lines with a marker once you open the shape out again, to show all the lines of symmetry you have found.

Three lines of symmetry

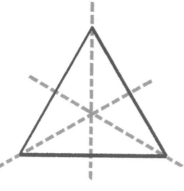

EQUILATERAL TRIANGLE

Four lines of symmetry

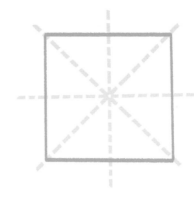

SQUARE

Five lines of symmetry

REGULAR PENTAGON

Six lines of symmetry

REGULAR HEXAGON

◎ ROTATIONAL SYMMETRY

A shape has rotational symmetry when it looks the same after a turn of less than 360°.

This shape has a rotational order of three because there are three turn positions in which the shape looks the same.

TESSELLATION

Do you have tiles on your kitchen or bathroom walls?
If you do, the pattern is an example of **tessellation**! Tessellation
is a pattern of 2D shapes that fit together with no gaps.

Squares, equilateral triangles, and hexagons all tessellate, as they fit together
perfectly. All the shapes do not need to be the same in a piece of tessellation,
but they do need to fit together without any gaps. The key to their tessellation
is that their vertices all add up to 360° around a given point.

 ## REGULAR TESSELLATION

In regular tessellation, all the shapes must be identical
regular polygons, like the hexagons in this patchwork.

OUT OF CURIOSITY

**The word tessellate comes
from the Latin word
tessellar, which was a small
piece of mosaic tiling!**

There are only three regular tessellations—a square,
a triangle, and a hexagon. For regular tessellation,
the pattern has to be the same at every vertex.

Here, the pattern is 6.6.6 because three hexagons
meet at each vertex, and hexagons have six sides.

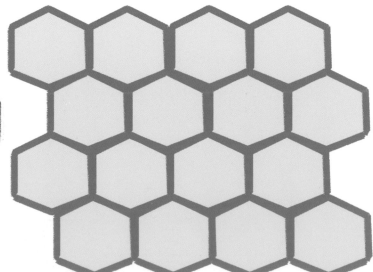

SEMI-REGULAR TESSELLATION

These floor tiles are an example of semi-regular tessellation.

In semi-regular tessellation, the tessellation can be made from two or more regular polygons, but the pattern at each vertex must be the same. To "name" the tessellation, you look at a vertex and write down how many sides each polygon has in order. You always start with the polygon with the least number of sides. These floor tiles show the patten 3.3.4.3.4

TYPES OF TESSELLATION

There are different types of tessellation. Reflection repeats shapes by reflecting them. Rotation repeats shapes by turning or rotating them. Translation repeats shapes by moving or sliding them.

DID YOU KNOW?

The artist M.C. Escher used tessellation in many of his paintings to great effect. The strange patterns create odd illusions.

TESSELLATION IN NATURE

It is fascinating to see tessellation in nature. Honeycomb, tortoise shell, and the pattern on giraffe skin all create tessellated patterns.

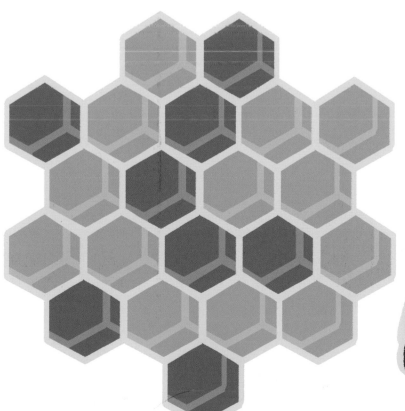

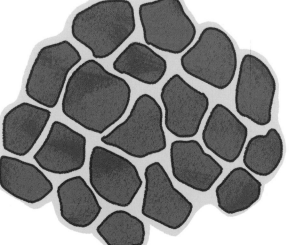

CHAPTER 4

MEASURE

We measure things to see how much they weigh, what size they are, and the passing of time. We measure things to organize our lives. We measure time using calendars and clocks.

We measure things using standard measures. If you go into a shop in Tokyo and buy a pound or kilogram of nuts, it will weigh the same as a pound or kilogram of nuts bought in London. We all know what a pound or kilogram "means."

A day lasts 24 hours, wherever you are in the world. Although time zones are different around the world, this helps people to organize meetings together, and coordinate their plans. School days, working hours, times of buses and trains—we need to measure time to organize life.

 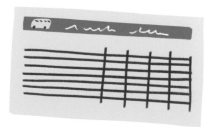

NON-STANDARD MEASURE

Non-standard measure is measurement using things such as hand spans or pencils to measure with instead of rulers and scales. It gives people a rough idea of measures and allows people to compare things—but it is not very accurate!

MEASUREMENT IN EARLY HISTORY

People have been measuring things for as long as there have been people! That does not mean there were always rulers and clocks, though—at least not as we know them. There is evidence from archeological digs to suggest that early people measured things such as the passing time with tally sticks. The first recorded systems of measurement appeared in ancient civilizations such as those in Mesopotamia, Egypt, and the Indus Valley. Different regions used different measures in farming, building, and trade. There were no worldwide "standard" measurements like we have today.

NON-STANDARD MEASURE

Even if you do not have a ruler, you can measure things. Imagine you wanted to measure a table and bench but you did not have a ruler handy. You could measure them in hand spans—or even with objects such as pencils!

You would have to place the pencils end to end to make sure there were no gaps. The table might be 10 pencils long and 6 pencils wide. If you measured the bench in the same way and it was 5 pencils long and 3 pencils wide, you would be able to compare the sizes of the two items (the bench is half as long and half as wide as the table) without actually knowing the measurements in centimeters or inches.

CUBITS AND BUSHELS

In ancient Egypt and Rome, people often measured length in cubits. These varied from place to place, but were often measured from the tip of the middle finger to the elbow, equal to two hand spans. Goods such as corn or flour were often measured by volume: the amount of seeds that fit in vessels. In medieval Europe, the measure of volume was often the bushel.

OUT OF CURIOSITY

The carat is a unit still used today for measuring gemstones. Originally, the unit of measure was the weight of a carob seed!

BODY-BASED MEASUREMENTS

King Henry I of England decided that a "yard" was the distance from his nose to his thumb on his outstretched arm! The thing is, not everyone has the same length arms, so that measure is non-standard. People also used to measure things in the length of a foot and the width of a finger. If you look around at your family and friends, you will easily see how this could be a problem as not all feet and fingers are the same size.

NON-STANDARD MEASUREMENT IN SCHOOLS TODAY

Young children are introduced to measuring length and weight with non-standard measure. Measuring things accurately is hard. Schools use non-standard measurement to teach young children about ideas such as "lighter," "heavier," "longer," and "shorter." Do you remember learning about measurement in this way?

STANDARD MEASURE

A standard measure is one that is exactly the same wherever you are in the world. It never varies and is measured accurately using instruments such as rulers, scales, clocks, and thermometers.

WHY USE STANDARD MEASUREMENTS?

When people around the world started trading with each other on a regular basis, they needed measurements everyone could understand. Local or non-standard measurements were no good as people in one country needed to know weights and measures that they were talking about when they made deals with people in other countries.

EARLY "STANDARD" MEASUREMENT

The ancient Egyptians, Romans, and Greeks used a "foot" as a measure—but these were not true standard measures as they were different lengths in different places. The Romans also introduced the "mile" or *mille passus* ("thousand paces"). This Roman mile spread across Europe as their armies invaded and occupied territories, including Britannia (modern Britain). The Roman mile was 5,000 Roman feet (around 4,859 feet or 1,481 m). In the 1500s, Queen Elizabeth 1 changed the length of a mile in England by law to be 5,280 feet.

OUT OF CURIOSITY

Before truly standard measure was introduced, there were many different strange measurements used, such as span, finger, nail, rod, pole, and perch!

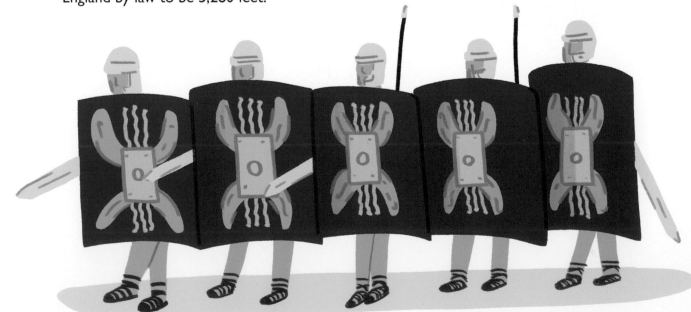

IMPERIAL AND US MEASUREMENT

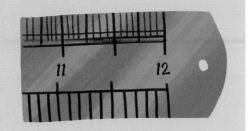

Imperial measurement is a type of standard measure that was used by the British Empire. The British Weights and Measures Act 1824 introduced the measures wherever Britain held control. Imperial measures are very similar to those used in the USA, as both systems are based on medieval English measurements.

In the last century, the UK and most other countries changed to the metric system (see below). The USA still uses its own customary **units**, such as pounds and ounces.

IMPERIAL AND US UNITS

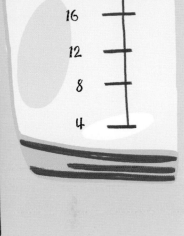

Length: inches, feet, yards, miles

Weight: ounces, pounds

Volume: fluid ounces, gills, pints, quarts, gallons

Area: acres, hectares

Temperature: degrees Fahrenheit

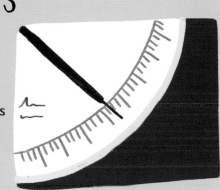

METRIC MEASUREMENT

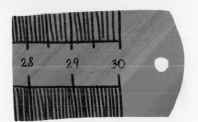

The metric system was adopted in France in 1799. It became the dominant system across the world by the end of the 20th century. The International System of Units is the modern metric system, agreed in 1960 by the General Conference on Weights and Measures. It has been adopted across the world except for in the USA, Liberia, and Myanmar.

METRIC UNITS

Length: millimeters, centimeters, meters, kilometers

Weight: grams, kilograms

Volume: milliliters, liters

Area: square centimeters, square kilometers

Temperature: degrees Celsius

MEASURING LENGTH AND DISTANCE

We label the measurements of a two-dimensional shape in length and width, with the larger dimension being called length—unless it's called height. Distance is measured between two points or objects. Length is measured as a dimension of a single object: We talk about the length of a line, for example.

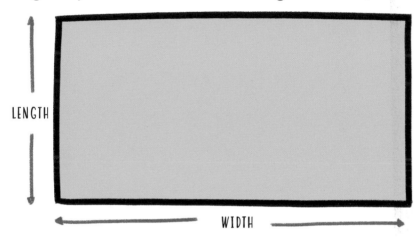

LENGTH

WIDTH

IMPERIAL AND US UNITS OF LENGTH

Length is measured in inches (in), feet (ft), yards (yd), and miles (mi). Inches are used to measure small things, like a pencil or an eraser. Feet, yards, and miles are used to measure larger things, like the distance between two places, such as home and school.

TOOLS FOR MEASURING LENGTH

Rulers and tape measures are used for measuring smaller items.

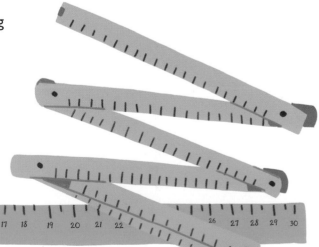

Short distances (in a garden or on a building site) may be measured with surveyor's wheels or a laser.

Look on the dashboard in a car to see an odometer. It shows the distance the car has driven.

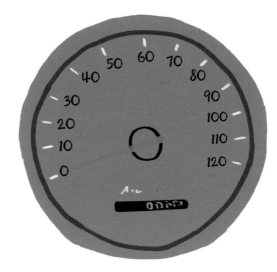

METRIC UNITS OF LENGTH

In the metric system of measure, it is easy to work out equivalent measures. One meter is the equivalent of 100 centimeters, for example. "Cent" comes from the Latin word for 100, and "centi" means "one-hundredth," which can help you to remember how many centimeters there are in a meter!

1 cm = 10 mm

1 m = 100 cm

1 km = 1,000 m

One kilometer is the equivalent of 1,000 meters. "Kilo" comes from the Greek word *kilo*, which means 1,000, which makes it easy to remember that there are 1,000 m in a km.

MAPS

A map that is drawn to **scale** helps us to work out the distance between two points. The scale tells us the ratio of a distance on the map to a distance on the ground. For example, in the metric system, a map scale of 1:50,000 means that 1 cm on the map is equal to 50,000 cm (or 500 m) on the ground. In the US and Imperial system, a scale of 1:63,360 means that 1 in on the map is equal to 63,360 in (or 1 mi) on the ground.

MEASURING WEIGHT

Have you ever lifted anything heavy or carried full shopping bags? Weight measures the force of **gravity** pulling down on an object. Gravity is the force that pulls objects toward each other. Earth's gravity keeps you on the ground rather than floating in the air! Gravity is the force that makes things fall to Earth when they are dropped. Gravity pulls harder on "heavy" things— and that's why they are harder to carry!

MASS

The weight of an object is a measure of the effect gravity has on its **mass**. On Earth, mass and weight are usually treated as the same and we report weight using the same units as we measure mass. A big, heavy rock has a lot of mass and a large weight. On the Moon, that rock would have the same mass but less weight, because the force of gravity on the Moon is smaller so it can't "pull" on the rock as hard.

WEIGHING THINGS UP

Scales and balances report weight in ounces (oz) and pounds (lb), or in the metric system, in grams (g) and kilograms (kg).

Milligrams (mg) are used for weighing tiny, light things, such as:

Grams or ounces are used for weighing small things. A paper clip weighs around 0.035 oz (1 g).

You may buy a bag of candy that weighs around 3.5 oz or 100 g.

Pounds or kilograms are used to weigh larger things, such as sacks of potatoes—or people!

US tons and metric tons are used to weigh heavy things, such as an elephant!

TOOLS FOR MEASURING WEIGHT

Weight is measured using scales:

Kitchen scales   Bathroom scales   Vehicle scales   Postal scales

METRIC CONVERSIONS

A milligram is 1,000th of a gram—there are 1,000 mg in 1 g.

There are 1,000 g in 1 kg.

There are 1,000 kg in 1 metric ton (1 t)

OUT OF CURIOSITY

If you weigh 32 kg (70.5 lb) on Earth, you would weigh around 77 kg (169.8 lb) on Jupiter—that's because of the force of gravity. Your weight would change due to the planet's different mass. Jupiter is a massive planet, and it has gravity around 2.4 times Earth's gravity.

Area is measured in square units. The area is the number of these squares that will fit inside the region being measured. In mathematics, area is used to measure shapes. In a real-life setting, area is used to measure rooms in houses, carpets, plots of land, and even whole countries!

FINDING AREA

If your backyard was a rectangle 7 m long and 5 m wide (or if you live in the USA, let's say 7 yards long and 5 yards wide), you multiply the length by the width to find the area.

$7 \times 5 = 35$, so the garden has an area of 35 m^2 (or 35 yards^2 if you're working in the USA).

7 M

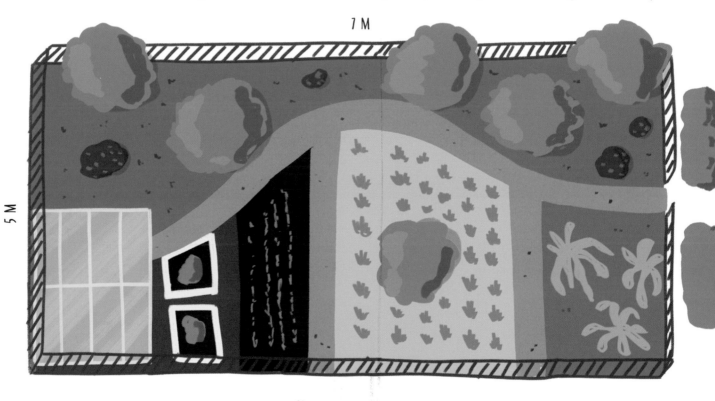

5 M

In the metric system, area is measured in square centimeters (cm^2), square meters (m^2), and square kilometers (km^2). In the US and Imperial systems, the measurements are in^2, ft^2, and mi^2.

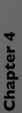

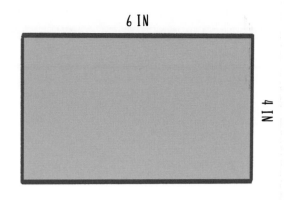

6 IN

4 IN

FINDING THE AREA OF A RECTANGLE

To find the area of a rectangle, you multiply the width by the height.

Area = width x height   A = w x h

The area of this rectangle is 6 in x 4 in = 24 in².

FINDING THE AREA OF A SQUARE

A square is a type of rectangle, but all sides of a square are the same length. To find the area of a square, multiply the length of two sides together.

The area of this square is 5 cm x 5 cm = 25 cm².

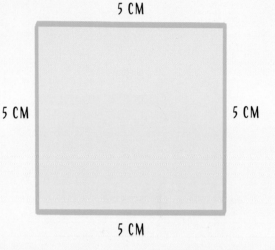

5 CM

5 CM

5 CM

5 CM

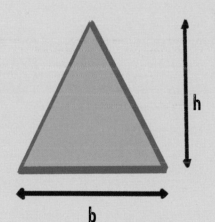

h

b

FINDING THE AREA OF A TRIANGLE

To find the area of a triangle, multiply half of the base measurement by the height measurement. If the base was 2 in and the height was 4 in, the area would be: ½ in x 2 in x 4 in = 4 in².

The formula is:

Area = ½ base x height   A = ½ x b x h

 # FINDING THE AREA OF A CIRCLE

To find the area of a circle we multiply pi x radius x radius.

Area = pi x radius x radius   A = π x r x r

Pi (see page 54) is equivalent to around 3.14. Imagine you want to find the area of a circle that has a radius of 2 cm. 2 x 2 is 4. So, the area is 3.14 x 4 = 12.56 cm².

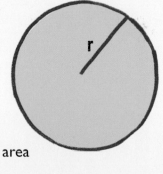

r

VOLUME AND CAPACITY

Volume is the amount of space an object takes up. A hollow object such as a jug or a box can hold a volume of something—a bottle might hold juice, for instance. The capacity of the object is the volume it can hold.

It is useful to measure volumes when you buy things like juice or milk by volume, and doctors work out the right volume of medicine to give you for your body size.

FINDING THE VOLUME OF CUBOIDS

The volume of cuboids can be found by measuring their height, width, and depth. To find the volume of a shape, you multiply length by height by width:

3 CM
3 CM
3 CM

$$V = length \; x \; height \; x \; width$$

$$V = l \; x \; h \; x \; w$$

The volume of this cuboid is 27 cm³.

UNITS OF MEASURING VOLUME AND CAPACITY

In metric, volume and capacity are measured in centimeters cubed (cm³), meters cubed (m³), milliliters (ml), centiliters (cl), and liters (l). In Imperial and US systems, volume and capacity are measures in fluid ounces, pints, and gallons.

OUT OF CURIOSITY

I centimeter cubed will hold I milliliter of liquid.

Think about the difference between capacity and volume. Capacity is a property of a container—it is the measure of space inside the container. Volume is the amount of liquid in the container.

TOOLS FOR MEASURING THE VOLUME OF LIQUIDS

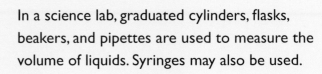

In a kitchen, measuring cups and measuring spoons are used to measure the volume of liquid ingredients.

In a science lab, graduated cylinders, flasks, beakers, and pipettes are used to measure the volume of liquids. Syringes may also be used.

Gas syringes may be used to measure the volume of gas produced in an experiment.

The gas (such as propane or butane) used in motorhomes for cooking is held in canisters or tanks that are measured in liters or gallons.

VOLUME OF POWDERS

In the kitchen, powders may be measured by measuring spoons or by "cups." Look at recipe books and see if you can find any recipes that call for a teaspoon of sugar or salt!

METRIC CONVERSIONS

There are 10 milliliters (ml) in a centiliter (cl) and 1,000 milliliters (ml) in a liter (l). There are 100 centiliters (cl) in a liter (l).

TIME

When we talk about the past, the present, and the future, we are talking about time. Telling the time helps us to organize our lives. It helps us to know when we should be at school, when to go to bed—and when it's meal time!

UNITS OF MEASURING TIME

Time is measured in seconds, minutes, hours, days, weeks, months, years, decades (10 years), centuries (100 years), and millennia (1,000 years).

TOOLS FOR MEASURING TIME

Time is measured with many tools, including watches, stopwatches, clocks, and calendars.

TELLING THE TIME BEFORE CLOCKS

Early people marked the passing of time by looking at the movement of the Sun, Moon, and stars in the sky, as well as noticing the changing seasons and when it was light and dark. Telling the time in this way helped them to plan trading journeys, hunts, farming, and festival days. The first "clocks" to mark the passing of time were stone placements, such as stone circles that mark when it is midsummer and midwinter by the changing position of the Sun in the sky through the year.

The Babylonians or Egyptians probably created the first true sundials by around 1500 BCE. These used the way the Sun seemed to move across the sky during the day to tell the time. As shadows were cast, the passing time was marked.

By around 1900 BCE, ancient Egyptians used obelisks, tall four-sided monuments, to tell the time. The length of the shadow cast, as well as its direction, could be used to tell time and season.

WATER CLOCKS AND HOURGLASSES

Water clocks are thought to be the earliest tools that did not use celestial bodies such as the Sun, Moon, or stars to calculate passing time. Water clocks mark time by water passing from one marked vessel to another. The ancient Greek inventor Ctesibius designed complex water clocks with dials and pointers.

Sandglasses may have been used by the Greeks in the 3rd century BCE. They were used in the Senate of ancient Rome to time speeches. Hourglasses became popular in medieval Europe. Hourglasses are two joined glass bulbs containing sand. They are turned upside down to allow the sand to pass from one bulb to another. The sand always takes the same amount of time to move, so an hourglass is useful for measuring a period of time, such as 1 hour.

"AM" AND "PM" AND THE 24-HOUR CLOCK

There are 24 hours in a day, which are often divided into two 12-hour periods. The first is "am"—this comes from the Latin *ante meridian*, which means before noon (midday). It runs from midnight to noon the next day. The second period is "pm"—it comes from the Latin *post meridian*. It runs from noon to midnight. In this system, the numbers 1 to 12 are used to tell the time. 3 am is early in the morning; 3 pm is in the afternoon.

The 24-hour clock does not use am and pm. Instead, it uses one 24-hour period. In some parts of the world, such as the USA, this is called "military time." Starting at midnight (00.00 hours), the clock moves through a 24-hour sequence. 3 in the morning is 03.00 hours; 3 in the afternoon is 15.00 hours.

COMPUTERS AND TIME

The clock time you see in the corner of your computer screen is probably the most accurate timekeeper in your house. It is synchronized with Internet time **servers**, which are very accurate. The "clock" in your computer keeps it running properly and helps it to stay updated. The "clock" is a **microchip** that regulates the timing and speed of all computer functions.

CALENDARS

Calendars mark the passing of time. We use calendars to organize our lives. We mark special dates such as birthdays and festivals on calendars. The calendar shows the days, weeks, and months as they pass.

Early calendars did not look like the calendars we hang on the wall today. Many were made of stone: Aztec calendars looked like beautiful stone-carved art!

MEGALITHS

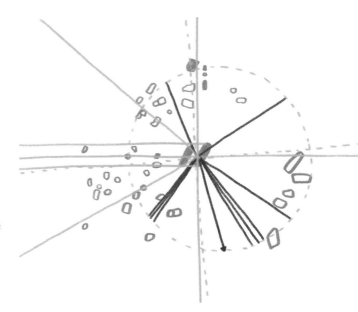

Megaliths are ancient stone structures. Some historians think the placement of the stones marked the movement of celestial bodies and acted as a calendar. The stone circles at the UK's Stonehenge, constructed between 3000 BCE and 2000 BCE, are believed to have acted as calendars. Particular stones framed the sunset and sunrise on the longest and shortest days of the year.

AZTEC CALENDAR

The Aztecs ruled parts of Mexico from the 14th to 16th centuries. They used two calendars that ran side by side. The **solar** calendar, Xiuhpohualli, lasted 365 days and was divided into 18 months of 20 days each, with 5 extra days at the end of the year. This calendar was used to mark the timing of things done during the agricultural year. The second calendar, Tonalpohualli, had 260 days. The Tonalpohualli was the sacred calendar that marked the timings of religious festivals.

LUNAR CALENDARS

A **lunar** calendar is based on the monthly cycle of the Moon as it moves from new moon to full moon and back again. The Moon seems to change shape in the night sky depending on how much of the part you see is facing the Sun. It is the Sun's light reflecting off the Moon that lets you see it.

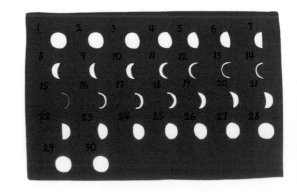

An ancient lunar calendar found at Warren Field in Scotland has been dated to 8000 BCE. It is made up of 12 pits. It is thought that hunters may have used the lunar calendar to plan hunts. Today, lunar calendars are still used to set the dates for religious festivals, such as Easter, Rosh Hashanah, Diwali, Chinese New Year, and Ramadan.

JULIAN CALENDAR

In early Roman times, a lunar calendar with 10 months was used. In 46 BCE, the Roman emperor Julius Caesar introduced the Julian calendar. This calendar had two different types of year—a year with 365 days and a "leap year" with 366 days. There was a cycle of three years followed by a **leap year**. Since the calendar (based on a 365-day year) did not keep pace with the true solar year (365.24 days), it got 3 days ahead every 400 years. The Julian calendar spread across the Roman Empire and was used widely until the Gregorian calendar (see left) was introduced. The Julian calendar is still used by the Eastern Orthodox Church.

GREGORIAN CALENDAR

The Gregorian calendar was introduced by Pope Gregory XIII in 1582. This reform of the Julian calendar did not change the months or the lengths of the months. It added the idea that any year with a number exactly divisible by 100 was not a leap year (except those years exactly divisible by 400). The change allowed the calendar to keep pace with the solar year. The Gregorian calendar still differs a little from astronomical time—but only by 1 day every 7,070 years!

HIJRI CALENDAR

In much of the Islamic world, the Gregorian calendar is used for most purposes, but the lunar Hijri calendar is used to work out the dates of religious festivals. The Hijri calendar has 12 months, but 354 or 355 days in each year. For the Gregorian calendar year 2021, the Hijri calendar year is for 1442–1443.

The months are called:

1. AL-MUHARRAM	7. RAJAB
2. SAFAR	8. SHA'BAN
3. RABI AL-AWWAL	9. RAMADAN
4. RABI ATH-THANI	10. SHAWWAL
5. JUMADA AL-ULA	11. DHU AL-QADAH
6. JUMADA AL-THANI	12. DHU AL-HIJJAH

CHINESE CALENDAR

Modern China uses the Gregorian calendar but it also uses the traditional Chinese lunisolar calendar (governed by the Sun and Moon) to mark festivals. This calendar developed between 771 and 476 BCE. It follows a 12-year cycle, each of those years represented by a different animal of the Chinese zodiac.

TIMETABLES AND ORGANIZATION

Timetables use mathematics to help us organize our lives!
They help us to plan appointments and journeys. They work alongside
calendars and clocks to make sure we are in the right place at the right time.

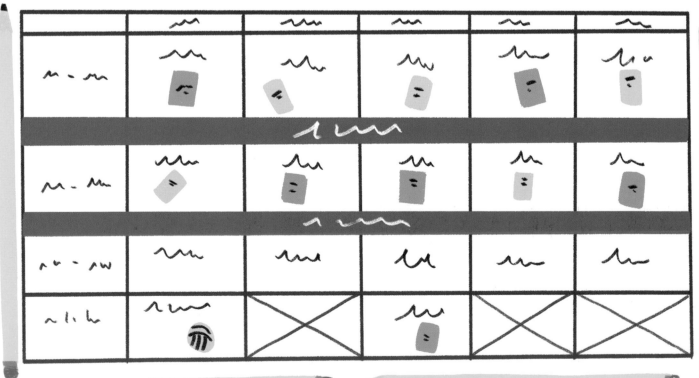

SCHOOL TIMETABLES

School timetables are needed so pupils and teachers know what classes to do at each time of the day. Without a timetable, it would be hard to plan activities or an order for people to use equipment at different times. In a school there may be one gym and one hall, for example—but may be six grade levels. Without a timetable, there would be chaos! Timetables like this help people to live alongside each other, sharing resources.

TIMETABLES FOR PLANNING JOURNEYS

Buses and trains have timetables to follow. Without them, traffic would get congested, and people would not know when to go to a bus stop or station to catch the bus or train they needed to get to their destination.

USING A TIMETABLE

Times on a timetable may look complicated, but they are really useful once you know how to use them. On this timetable, if you wanted to catch a bus from Tower Bridge to Westminster, you would look down the list to find Tower Bridge. Once you have found it, read along the line to see the times the bus stops at Tower Bridge. On this timetable it says the bus stops there at 8:48, 10:14, 11:59, and 13:59. To catch the bus at the Tower Bridge stop, you would have to be at the stop at one of those times—the bus won't wait!

BUS STOPS	DAILY TIMES			
St Paul's Cathedral	08:34	10:00	11:45	13:45
Tower of London	08:46	10:12	11:57	13:57
Tower Bridge	08:48	10:14	11:59	13:59
The Shard	08:56	10:22	12:07	14:07
Tate Modern	09:03	10:29	12:14	14:14
London Eye	09:12	10:38	12:23	14:23
Westminster	09:17	10:43	12:28	14:28
Downing Street	09:23			
Buckingham Palace	09:30			

You can then find out how long it will take for the bus to arrive at Westminster by reading down the timetable to find the Westminster stop. If you caught the 8:48 bus from Tower Bridge, it would get to Westminster at 9:17. If you subtract the time you left (8:48) from the time you arrive (9:17), you can see that the journey takes 29 minutes.

FIRST TIMETABLE

The first known published train timetable was *Bradshaw's Railway Time Tables and Assistant to Railway Travelling*, printed in 1839 in England. Since there was no standardized time in England, all times given were London time, which was 18 minutes ahead of Exeter time. In 1880, standardized time was adopted across Great Britain to solve such problems.

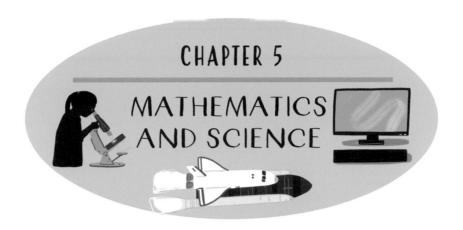

CHAPTER 5

MATHEMATICS AND SCIENCE

Mathematics and science go hand in hand. Without mathematics, we would not be able to measure or calculate the results of experiments.

Mathematics is everywhere. STEM stands for science, technology, engineering, and mathematics. STEM education is an important part of school learning because it is the basis for many important jobs, from bridge-building to perfume-testing. Without mathematics, science, technology, and engineering would not "work"—there would be no way to measure out materials, figure out angles, measure lengths, time projects, and make **equations** to solve problems!

Without mathematics, there would be no computers or **artificial intelligence** (AI). Mathematics is used in coding, and computing helps mathematics in turn. Sets of rules called **algorithms** are being used by computers to solve complex mathematical problems.

There would be no space travel without mathematics to help build rockets and measure **forces** like thrust, which lifts rockets into the air. Without mathematics there would be no machines invented or built for industry.

Without mathematics, medicine as we know it would not exist. Probability and collected statistics and other data help to work out if new drugs are effective. They also help to work out the effectiveness of surgery in making people better. Mathematics is used to measure out dosages of medicine. It is also used to calculate the right amount of a substance needed to put people to sleep during operations. Without mathematics, there would be no devices, such as X-ray machines, that are used by doctors to diagnose and treat illnesses.

MEDICINE MATHEMATICS

Doctors, nurses, and surgeons use mathematics every day to keep us healthy and to save lives. Health professionals use mathematics when they work out the dosage of prescriptions we need for life-saving drugs, and we use mathematics when we measure out the doses to take the medicine.

PRESCRIPTIONS

Most medicines are given with a dosage in milligrams (mg) per kilogram (kg). Doctors use mathematics to figure out the size of the dose needed according to a patient's weight. Veterinarians also do this when they treat our pets.

Doctors use mathematics to figure out how many times a day medication needs to be taken for the right dosage, and then how many tablets are needed for a course of treatment.

Doctors need to be able to figure out how long the medicine stays in the patient's body before they need another dose. If they do not do this, the patient could end up with too much medicine in their body and that could be bad for their health. The amount of medicine in the patient's body decreases by a percentage each hour. This is a decrease that can be predicted and mapped over time.

X-RAYS AND CAT SCANS

Mathematics is used to build, run, and interpret the readings from machines used to give X-rays and CAT (Computerized Axial Tomography) scans. X-rays take 2D pictures of the inside of our bodies, showing things like broken bones. CAT scans give a 3D image and can look inside organs such as the brain. A CAT scanner takes hundreds of pictures at different angles, then a computer uses mathematical algorithms to put the pictures together into a 3D image. Doctors use such images to check for any problems so they can be treated.

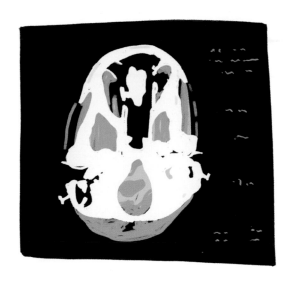

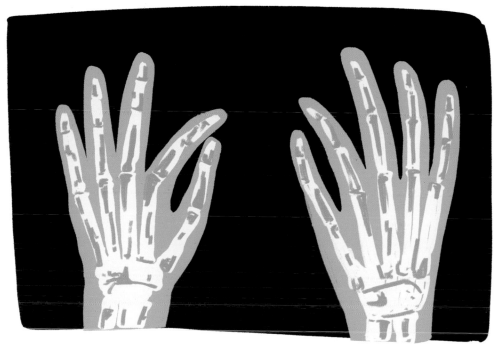

SMASHING STONES

A lithotripter uses shock waves to shatter kidney stones and gallstones, which are solid pieces of material that develop inside the body. Without this treatment, people need surgery. How does mathematics make this possible?

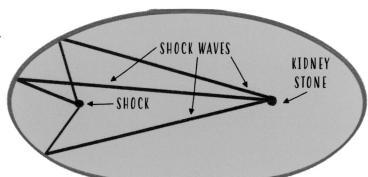

SHOCK WAVES

KIDNEY STONE

SHOCK

The surgeon places the lithotripter, which is shaped as half an ellipsoid (3D ellipse), on the patient's body. The lithotripter blasts out ultrasound waves (sound waves that humans cannot hear), which reflect off the inside surface of the ellipsoid to come together on the stone. All the waves focus on the stone and have enough energy to blast it apart. The patient can go home about an hour later.

MATHEMATICS AND INFECTIOUS DISEASES

Mathematics is used by scientists called epidemiologists to track the spread and progress of **infectious** diseases. This helps to manage the health of groups of people, and to model the potential outcome of an **epidemic** or **pandemic**, such as the outbreak of COVID-19. Mathematics can also calculate the effects of **vaccination** programs.

TRANSMISSION AND SPREAD OF DISEASE

Epidemiologists use mathematical models to project how quickly and how far an infectious disease is likely to spread as it is passed from person to person. This information can be used to help make health policies, such as whether a **quarantine** is needed in a particular area.

SIR MODEL

The SIR mathematical model was created in 1927 to study the spread of infectious diseases in a group of people. SIR stands for susceptible (who can catch the disease), infected (who is capable of spreading the disease), and recovered (who is immune because they have recovered or been vaccinated). The numbers generated are then multiplied, depending on what fraction the studied group is of the whole population. SIR is used in the study of illnesses such as measles, mumps, and rubella, which the MMR vaccination protects against.

R NUMBERS

You may have heard people talking about the R number when they discussed COVID-19. The R number is the reproduction number.

The R number is a way to measure how transferable a disease is from person to person. It is the average number of people that an infectious person will infect. The R number tells us whether an infection will die out, spread quickly, or stay constant. If the R number is greater than 1, the disease will spread. The higher the R number, the more a disease is spreading. Each infected person infects more so the disease multiplies.

If the R number is equal to 1, the disease will keep moving through the population but will not increase or decrease numbers of infected people at any given time. If the R number is less than 1 it means each infected person passes the disease to less than 1 person, so the disease dies out. The R number helps policy makers decide on a course of action such as quarantine and vaccination programs.

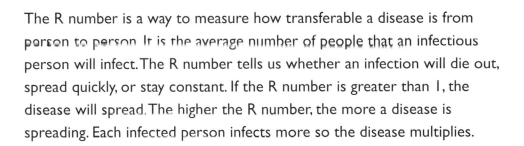

R = 1

R = 2.5

SUMS FOR SURGERY

Surgeons and anesthesiologists use mathematics when people need surgery. Without their calculations, people would not be safe when they had operations—so mathematics saves lives!

MATHEMATICAL MODELS IN SURGERY

A mathematical model is a description of a system using mathematical ideas and language. Mathematical models can help surgeons to understand processes and predict the outcomes of different actions that they may take. This makes it more likely that an operation will have a good outcome, and the person having the operation will have their health improved and will recover well.

BRAIN SURGERY

Brain surgery is delicate and difficult—but mathematicians have found a way to make it a little safer. Mathematics can now be used to model and study the brain at the level of cells, and computer **simulations** use mathematics to show the success of a given type of surgery.

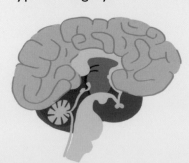

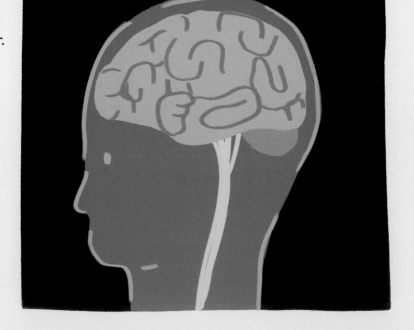

❤ HEART SURGERY

Surgeons operating on hearts use mathematics to help them to get the results they want—a healthy, working heart. They use symmetry to repair the ventricles in hearts as they reconstruct damaged parts.

Surgeons can model the geometry of the individual patient's heart and try out different possible structures on the model so they pick the best one to direct the surgery.

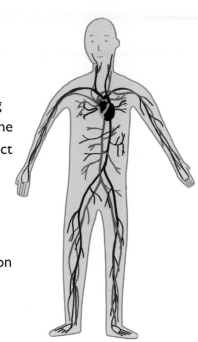

❤ ANESTHESIA

When you have an operation, you are not aware of what is going on, and you feel no pain. This is because you have been put to sleep with drugs. These might be injected, or given as a gas you breathe. The anesthesiologist uses mathematics to calculate how much of the drug you need to keep you asleep during the operation.

THE MATHEMATICS OF WEATHER FORECASTS

Have you ever looked at a weather forecast to see if it will be sunny enough for a picnic? Then say thanks to mathematics! It has been used to predict the weather since the 1920s.

NUMERICAL WEATHER PREDICTION

In the 1920s, a Norwegian meteorologist (a scientist who studies the weather) named Vilhelm Bjerknes developed an equation that helped to predict weather patterns. This was the beginning of modern weather forecasting.

In 1922, English mathematician Lewis Fry Richardson created a method to use mathematics to solve equations to predict the weather. He came up with the idea of a "forecast factory"—a huge building where people would use walls painted to show all of the countries in the world, and where up to 64,000 people would carry out calculations. In reality, more than a million people would be needed. Richardson's idea did not work in practical terms, but it paved the way for the use of **supercomputers** to predict the weather.

COMPUTING WEATHER PATTERNS

By the 1950s, computers could use mathematical models to predict weather with some accuracy. Today, supercomputers use data collected by satellites around the globe—but they are still able to predict only around six days ahead as things change so quickly. Any slight error in a calculation can make a massive difference to the results and in turn the prediction.

OUT OF CURIOSITY

In the 1950s, mathematician John von Neumann, who had worked on the creation of nuclear weapons, worked on ways how weather prediction could use weather as a weapon. The project failed.

ENSEMBLE FORECASTS

The huge number of variables (changeable things) in weather forecasting prevents exact predictions. Variables include:

Solar radiation

The power of the Sun's rays depends on cloud cover.

Precipitation

Water falls as rain, sleet, snow, and hail.

Soil

Soil moisture affects weather forecasts due to **evaporation**.

Vegetation

Plants release water into the air.

Surface water

Oceans and lakes release heat more slowly than land.

Terrain

Mountains affect rain and wind.

As a result of these variables, ensemble weather forecasts are created. This means that a set of weather forecasts are used to predict the range of weather that can be expected.

DATA COLLECTION

Observational data (information collected from watching and measuring things) is collected in a variety of ways.

Weather balloons rise into the troposphere, the lowest layer of Earth's atmosphere, where most weather conditions occur. The balloons carry devices called radiosondes that measure conditions, and transmit them to a receiver. Weather satellites collect and transmit data. Special planes also collect data by flying around weather systems such as tropical cyclones, and across the oceans, looking at sea ice. Weather stations around the world measure conditions and collect data.

Supercomputers process the data using algorithms. The computer at the Met Office in the UK can perform more than 16,000 trillion calculations per second. This helps to make weather forecasts more accurate—and it's all down to mathematics!

THE MATHEMATICS OF CLIMATE CHANGE

The climate changes naturally over time, but in the last century the speed of change has been dramatic, largely due to burning **fossil fuels** in factories and cars, which releases greenhouse gases. Greenhouse gases, such as carbon dioxide, keep the Earth warm and allow living things to survive by trapping the Sun's heat in the atmosphere. Too much greenhouse gas traps too much heat, so the temperature of the air and ocean rises.

Mathematics helps scientists to measure rates of change and to collect and process data that governments can use to create policies to combat climate change.

RISING TEMPERATURES

The world's temperatures have risen enough to cause the melting of polar ice caps and the slow rising of sea levels. This destroys habitat for polar bears and other animals. It also causes flooding of coastal areas used for houses and farming.

DATA HANDLING AND STATISTICS

"Climate" means the average weather conditions over a period of time. Scientists collect data about temperature, rainfall, sea level, and air pollution. This data is used to find out the average conditions. Keeping records and studying the change in these averages helps scientists to see if there are any changes or trends.

PROBABILITY

Mathematicians use probability to predict changing weather patterns caused by rising temperatures, such as floods and heatwaves that can lead to drought and wildfires. This can help governments to plan action to respond to the problems and may also influence them to change policy to reduce the burning of fossil fuels.

THE FOOD INDUSTRY

The food industry is the name given to the collection of many different businesses, including factories, that process and produce food. Climate change can affect the food industry because it relies on agriculture (farming crops and breeding animals for food), which is affected by problems such as drought and flooding. The predictions made by mathematicians about climate change can help the food industry to prepare for the future.

MATHEMATICS AND GREEN ENERGY

Renewable energy sources such as wind and water power can help to reduce the production of the greenhouse gases that accelerate climate change. Mathematical models can help with activities such as figuring out how many wind turbines are needed to power cities.

THE MATHEMATICS OF EARTHQUAKES

Earthquakes can cause loss of life and huge amounts of damage. Scientists use **lasers** to measure ground movement and their calculations help them to predict when an earthquake might be likely to happen. This helps to keep people out of danger zones. They also use mathematics to measure earthquakes as they happen.

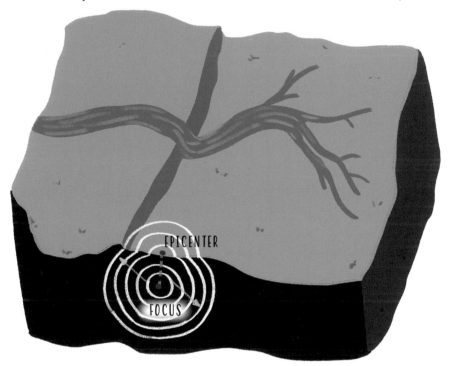

LAYERS OF THE EARTH

The Earth has layers—the inner core, outer core, mantle, and crust. The crust is made up of pieces (called tectonic plates) which move very slowly. Earthquakes happen when the edges of a plate get stuck but the rest of the plate keeps moving. When the edges come unstuck and the energy of the moving plate is released suddenly, there is an earthquake.

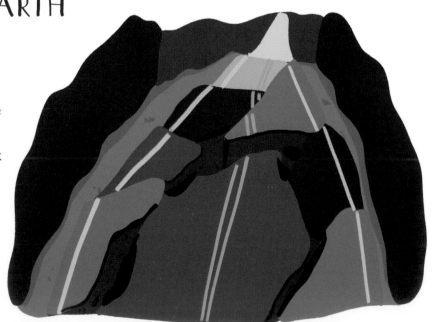

SEISMIC WAVES

The energy moves outward in **seismic waves**. The waves shake the ground and, when they reach the surface, buildings can crumble. Seismic waves are measured on instruments called seismographs. Sometimes the earthquake happens under the ocean floor and causes a series of large waves called a tsunami.

MAGNITUDE

The size of an earthquake is called the magnitude—it measures the strength of its seismic waves. Magnitude can be measured on scales such as the Richter scale or Moment Magnitude scale. The Richter scale is a measurement of the energy released by an earthquake. Earthquakes with a magnitude of 8 or above are thankfully rare as they destroy anything at the epicenter. In 2004, an earthquake of 9.1–9.3 on the Richter scale took place off the coast of Indonesia, setting off a deadly tsunami.

THE EPICENTER

The epicenter of an earthquake is the point directly above the focus of the earthquake. Scientists use mathematics to find the epicenter. They measure and chart the seismic waves' primary and secondary waves. The time between the primary and secondary waves tells the scientists the distance the seismometer measuring the waves is from the earthquake epicenter.

They **triangulate** three distances to find the earthquake's epicenter. On this map, circles are drawn around three seismometers. Each circle has a radius that matches the distance to the epicenter. The point where the circles intersect (overlap each other) is the epicenter of the earthquake.

COMPUTERS

Do you use a computer, smartphone, or tablet? Maybe you use a computer to do homework, play games, or talk to your friends? Perhaps your family shops or takes classes online. Without mathematics, there would be no computers—so no Internet!

THE HISTORY OF COMPUTERS

The first computer scientists were mathematicians. Look at this timeline of computing to discover the links between mathematics and computing.

1822 English mathematician Charles Babbage invents a steam-powered calculating machine that can compute tables of numbers.

1936 Alan Turing invents the "automatic machine" (later called the Turing machine). This machine is the forerunner of modern computers.

1941 J.V. Atanasoff invents a computer that can solve 29 equations at the same time. This is the first computer that can store information in its main memory.

1943 Colossus at Bletchley Park is used to help break enemy codes during World War II.

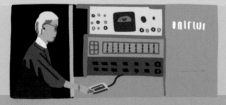

1945 Mauchly and Eckert build the Electronic Numerical Integrator and Calculator (ENIAC), which is seen as the "grandfather" of digital computers. Unlike the slim laptops, PCs, and smartphones of today, this monster machine fills a room!

1955 Grace Hopper helps to develop an early computer "language"—used to convert instructions that humans write into numbers that computers read.

1958 Jack Kilby and Robert Noyce invent the integrated circuit—the **computer chip**.

1964 Douglas Engelbart introduces a **prototype** of the modern computer with a mouse and easy-to-use menus, called a graphical user interface.

1971 Alan Shugart at IBM invents the "floppy disk," allowing data to be shared between computers. Before that, data was stored on tape, and before that on punched cards.

1975 Bill Gates and Paul Allen write **software** for the Altair 8800. The friends launch their own software company, called Micro-Soft at the time.

1976 Steve Jobs and Steve Wozniak start Apple Computers, inventing the Apple 1, the first computer with a single **circuit board**.

1981 IBM works on Acorn, and launches the IBM PC (personal computer).

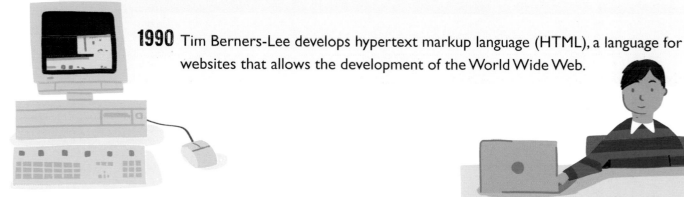

1990 Tim Berners-Lee develops hypertext markup language (HTML), a language for websites that allows the development of the World Wide Web.

BINARY AND CODING

The binary number system uses the numerals 0 and 1. This system is used by computers, with the numbers working as a series of on and off switches. Data in computers is stored and sent in binary.

MORE MATHEMATICS

In nearly every computer program everywhere, addition, subtraction, multiplication, and division are used to create **functions** in the program.

Algebra is used in the creation of software, and statistics is used for speech recognition, computer simulations, and artificial intelligence (AI). AI is when a computer **program** has the ability to learn from previous results so it seems to "think."

Calculus (which is a type of mathematics that studies rates of change) is used to create graphs and visuals, as well as being used for problem solving.

THE MATHEMATICS OF FLIGHT

Aeronautical engineering is the design of things that move through air, such as helicopters, planes, and drones. Aerospace engineering is the design of things that fly through space, like spacecraft and satellites. Both of these types of engineering use mathematics to make things move through the air.

 ## ENGINEERING

Engineers use mathematics to work out how to build aircraft that can travel at speed and carry loads (including passengers) safely. They need to use geometry to work out the most aerodynamic (able to fly easily) shapes for parts of the aircraft. They also need to use algebra to solve equations to make sure aircraft can fly safely as they are buffeted by wind. Engineers use computer science to help them design and develop aircraft—and to test and control them.

✈ PILOTS

Pilots use mathematics to plan and follow routes. When you go on vacation, the pilot is working with geometry at the front of the plane! Pilots read compasses and calculate angles to ensure they turn the plane correctly to stay on course.

Pilots read information from computers to help them make safe flights. The computers use mathematics to make sure there is enough fuel for the flight. They also work out if the plane is carrying too much weight to take off and land safely. That is why there are "baggage allowances" when you go on vacation—to make sure the plane can fly safely and has enough fuel.

✈ IT'S ROCKET SCIENCE!

Mathematics is key to space travel. Astronauts rely on computers that use mathematics to calculate distance, speed, and velocity (how fast something moves in a particular direction) to make sure they are able to launch and fly their spacecraft safely, and later to re-enter Earth's atmosphere and land safely.

For a rocket to be sent into space, the amount of fuel required must be calculated exactly. There is an equation called the rocket equation that tells engineers how to calculate the speed gained by a rocket as it burns its fuel. The mathematics needs to be accurate for the right amount of fuel to be used for a flight.

OUT OF CURIOSITY

The mathematical study of how objects move in the Solar System is called celestial mechanics—that sounds heavenly!

THE MATHEMATICS OF WORMHOLES

A wormhole is the name given to a possible passage through space that creates a shortcut through time and space. It would be like a tunnel that has its ends in two different points in space and time. We do not yet truly know if wormholes exist, but scientists are studying the idea to see if it can be proven.

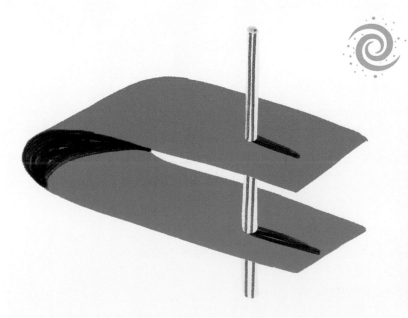

UNDERSTANDING WORMHOLES

To be able to understand wormholes, a 3D model might help you. Take a sheet of paper and curve (rather than fold) it over across the middle, so the two ends are touching. If a small hole is cut in either side of the paper, and a straw is poked through both, that is a 3D model of a wormhole.

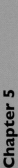

AN IDEA DEVELOPS

In 1921, Hermann Weyl began the study of wormholes as an idea. In 1935, Albert Einstein and Nathan Rosen began to study the idea of "bridges" through space-time, which would connect to different points via a shortcut. They used complicated mathematical formulas to develop their theories. The bridges they studied became known as Einstein-Rosen bridges—or wormholes.

In the 1980s, the study of wormholes was developed by Kip Thorne, an astrophysicist (space scientist) at the California Institute of Technology (Caltech). He researched theories about wormholes and the possibility of travel through them after talking to his friend Carl Sagan. Sagan was writing a science fiction book called *Contact* and he wanted to see if the type of space travel he was writing about might be possible.

Thorne and his colleagues looked at the idea of time travel via wormholes. They studied the idea of speeding up the entrance to a wormhole to the speed of light. They came to the conclusion that, if this were possible (and it's a big "if"), the high-speed mouth of the wormhole could maybe experience 1 year passing for every 100 years at the other mouth. That would make time travel potentially possible!

WORMHOLES IN SCIENCE FICTION

Wormholes pop up often in science fiction stories because these possibly fictional "bridges" allow fast travel across universes. They are even used for time-traveling stories, where people enter one end of the wormhole in one time period and exit in another entirely! It is an exciting thought, but it may only be make believe.

WORMHOLES TODAY

So far, no evidence of wormholes has been found. Scientists, with the help of mathematics, are still exploring the idea that these amazing shortcuts could be used to travel through time!

CHAPTER 6

THE ROCK STARS OF MATHEMATICS

Without mathematicians to develop and explain mathematics, where would we be? In trouble! Over the centuries, great thinkers have worked out all of the mathematics we use today. We know that mathematics is important—but who were those incredible people who made everything possible?

There have been many people through the ages from all parts of the world who have shaped mathematics. It is hard to decide who has made the most important discoveries and theories. The people in this chapter have all played an important part in the mathematics we use today.

We know a lot about the lives of some of these people and less about others. Some made world-changing mathematical discoveries and others made the world of mathematics more accessible to everyone. They all have one thing in common: They had or have brilliant minds.

PYTHAGORAS
c.570-c.495 BCE, GREECE

Pythagoras was a Greek philosopher and mathematician. He was born on the Greek island of Samos in around 570 BCE. He traveled as a young man, possibly getting his education in Egypt and Babylon before returning to Greece.

Pythagoras believed that numbers formed the basis of all things. He is best known for his Pythagorean Theorem. It says that when a triangle has a right angle, and squares are made on each of the three sides, the biggest square has the same area as the other two squares combined—amazing!

It can be written in this way:
$$a^2 + b^2 = c^2$$

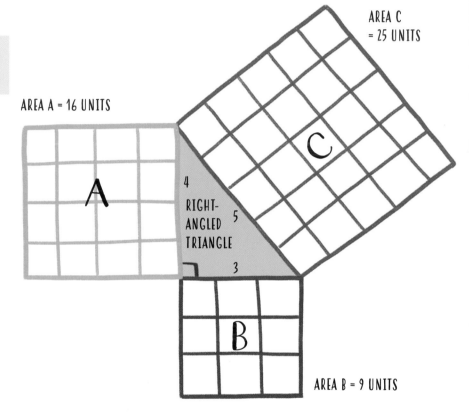

AREA C = 25 UNITS

AREA A = 16 UNITS

C

A

4

RIGHT-ANGLED TRIANGLE

5

3

B

AREA B = 9 UNITS

There is some evidence to suggest that the Babylonians may have created the theorem long before Pythagoras, and that he may have learned about it during his studies there.

Pythagoras left Samos again when he was around 40 years old. He moved to Croton in southern Italy, which at the time was a Greek colony. There he created a school so he could share his beliefs and educate others.

HYPATIA
c.360-415 CE, EGYPT

Hypatia was born in Alexandria some time between the year 350 CE and 370 CE. She was a mathematician and astronomer. At the time Hypatia lived, Alexandria was a city of scholars. Her father, Theon, was a mathematician. This gave Hypatia the perfect place to build her education, learning from the clever people around her. While growing up, Hypatia began to work with her father and was even said to have produced some of his work!

At the height of Hypatia's career she was described as the world's leading mathematician. She was a naturalist (someone who studies plants and animals), a physicist (someone who studies matter and energy), and a feminist (someone who supports women's rights) as well as an inventor and astronomer. She was also a great sportsperson, wonderful at running and swimming.

Hypatia created commentaries on the work of other mathematicians. This means that she discussed their work and its meaning, adding more ideas. This was vital as it allowed the knowledge within the works to spread further as it was discussed by more students of mathematics.

In 400 CE, Hypatia became head of a school in Alexandria. She proved herself to be a great teacher and philosopher (someone who discusses ideas). However, her ideas led to her death. Alexandria's rulers were Christian, but Hypatia was not. Her religious views made her a target.

In 415 CE, she was attacked by a political or religious mob. They killed her and her brilliant mind was lost to the world.

AL-KHWARIZMI
c.780-c.850 CE, UZBEKISTAN

Muhammad ibn Musa al-Khwarizmi was a Persian mathematician, astronomer, and geographer. He is known as the "father of algebra." He was born in Khwarezm (now Uzbekistan) in around 780 CE.

Al-Khwarizmi worked at Baghdad's House of Wisdom, a great academy and library where books were translated. In around 820 CE, he was appointed the astronomer and head of the library of the academy.

His book *The Science of Restoring and Balancing (Ilm al-Jabr wal-Muqabala)* provided methods to solve complex equations. The Arabic words *al-jabr* mean "restoring broken parts." This led to this field of mathematics being known as algebra. The word entered the English language in the 15th century, but this referred to setting broken bones! The first time it was used in English to describe mathematics was in the 16th century.

Al-Khwarizmi also studied trigonometry, which is the study of the sides and angles of triangles. He described the movements of the Sun, Moon, and known planets.

He is thought to have stayed in Iraq until his death in around 850 CE.

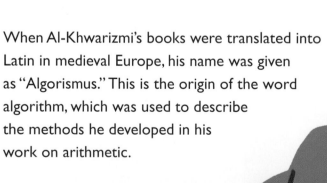

When Al-Khwarizmi's books were translated into Latin in medieval Europe, his name was given as "Algorismus." This is the origin of the word algorithm, which was used to describe the methods he developed in his work on arithmetic.

Al-Khwarizmi used the Indo-Arabic number system. This spread to Europe in the 12th century, and had a large impact on European mathematics.

OMAR KHAYYAM
1048-1131, IRAN

Omar Khayyam was born in 1048 in the city of Nishapur in Khorasan, which is now in Iran.

At around the age of 20, Khayyam went to the city of Samarkand, which is now in Uzbekistan in central Asia, to work in the king's treasury. He wrote about arithmetic, algebra, and music theory. He is also known for his work applying algebra to geometry.

In Samarkand, Khayyam was treated with great respect by the ruler. He was put in charge of the **observatory** at Isfahan in Iran, where he accurately measured the length of a year. His Jalali calendar is said to be more accurate than the Gregorian calendar most of the world uses today. It was used in Iran until the 20th century.

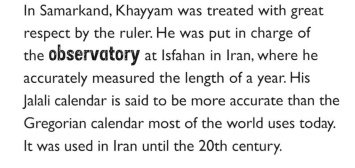

Omar Khayyam died at the age of 83 in 1131, in his home town of Nishapur. Since his death, his work as a poet has become well known. English poet Edward FitzGerald translated his poems in 1859, calling the collection *The Rubaiyat of Omar Khayyam*.

GIROLAMO CARDANO
1501-1576, ITALY

Girolamo Cardano was born in 1501 in Pavia in northern Italy. He studied medicine at the University of Pavia, then when the university closed due to the Four Years' War in Italy, he moved to Padua. Here he argued with lots of people and did not make friends easily. He moved to Saccolungo to get married, then moved to Milan with his new family.

Cardano worked as a lecturer of mathematics at the Piatti Foundation, and joined the College of Surgeons. From this point on he worked in both mathematics and medicine. As a mathematician, Cardano worked with negative numbers and probability.

His knowledge of probability helped him to successfully gamble, which at some points in his life was his main source of income. He wrote a book, *Book on Games of Chance*, which is as known as the earliest treatment of probability and an important mathematical method called **calculus**.

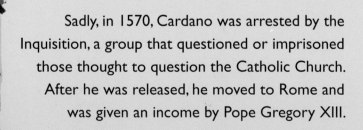

Sadly, in 1570, Cardano was arrested by the Inquisition, a group that questioned or imprisoned those thought to question the Catholic Church. After he was released, he moved to Rome and was given an income by Pope Gregory XIII.

Cardano worked as a mathematician and physician in Rome until his death in 1576.

ISAAC NEWTON
1642-1727, UK

Born on Christmas day in 1642, Newton went to school at The Kings School in Grantham but did not work very hard at first! At 17, his widowed mother took him out of school to manage her farm, Woolsthorpe Manor.

Luckily, Newton's uncle William convinced his mother that it would be better for Newton to return to school. Now he worked hard enough to continue his education at Trinity College, Cambridge. In 1665, the Great Plague sent him home for safety. It was during this break that he worked on a groundbreaking theory about gravity.

Newton returned to Cambridge after the plague. Now he proved that white light can be split into a rainbow of shades, which he demonstrated by viewing light through a prism. This led to Newton's Theory of Color. He constructed the first reflecting telescope in 1668, using mirrors rather than lenses to focus light.

In 1678, Newton suffered a breakdown and withdrew from public life. In 1684, the astronomer Edmund Halley (who studied and named Halley's Comet) visited Newton. Halley suggested Newton organize his own notes, and in 1687 Newton published a three-book collection that contained his Laws of Motion (describing the relationship between the motion of an object and the forces acting on it) and his Law of Universal Gravitation.

In 1689, Newton became the Member of Parliament for Cambridge University. He moved back to London in 1696 and became Master of the Royal Mint. He investigated counterfeiting (faking) of silver coins.

When Newton died in 1727, his work had helped to lay a foundation for much of the science we use today.

LEONHARD EULER
1707-1783, SWITZERLAND

Leonhard Euler was born in 1707 in Basel, Switzerland. He went to university when he was only 13 years old.

In 1727, Euler moved to St. Petersburg, in Russia, to teach medicine at the Academy of Sciences. He also worked as a medic in the Russian Navy. He soon moved to the mathematics department.

Euler moved to Berlin in 1741 to teach at the Berlin Academy. He spent the next 25 years of his life there continuing his work in mathematics. He published books about functions and calculus (calculating rates of change).

In 1766, Euler returned to Russia. He began to work with his sons, perhaps as a result of his poor eyesight. After a sickness in 1738, his vision had started to fail. By 1771 he was completely blind.

Euler died in 1783. He had worked in many areas of mathematics, including geometry, algebra, **number theory**, and trigonometry. In calculus, he even has a number named after him, Euler's number, which is around 2.71828.

CARL GAUSS
1777-1855, GERMANY

Born in April 1777, Johann Carl Friedrich Gauss had a remarkable ability to recognize patterns in numbers. One story says that, aged three, he corrected his father's calculations. Another says that he was punished in school for being naughty by being given a page of calculations—and he gave the answers in seconds!

In 1788, the Duke of Brunswick heard about the clever 11-year-old Gauss. The duke paid for him to attend college and, later, the university at Göttingen.

Gauss made his first major discovery while studying at Göttingen. He proved that a regular polygon with 17 sides could be drawn with a ruler and a compass. This was an important discovery because it helped prove a deep connection between algebra and geometry. Gauss wrote about number theory and brought together other theories, filling gaps.

The discovery of the dwarf planet Ceres by Giuseppe Piazzi in 1801 was thrilling. However, Piazzi could not track the movement of Ceres long enough to predict its pattern before it got lost behind the Sun. Gauss worked out a method to say when Ceres would reappear.

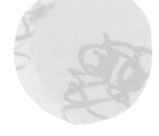

In 1807, Gauss become head of the observatory at Göttingen. In 1818, he invented the heliotrope—an instrument that uses a mirror to reflect sunlight over great distances to measure positions.

Gauss died in 1855 at the age of 78. He had contributed to algebra, number theory, geometry, astronomy, **mechanics**, and more.

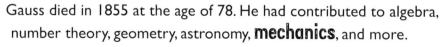

GEORG CANTOR
1845-1918, RUSSIA

Georg Cantor was born in Russia, but moved to Germany when he was 11. He was brilliant at mathematics and became a professor at the University of Halle when he was 34.

Cantor wrote about number theory and calculus. Perhaps his most important work, though, was on infinity. He could be called the first mathematician who really understood what infinity means in mathematical terms. Until the end of the 19th century, infinity was an idea—but just that it was a value that could never be found.

Georg Cantor took this abstract idea and made it more concrete. He developed set theory, the study of groups of objects (either real or purely mathematical), which is one of the building blocks of modern mathematics.

Cantor's mental illness led him to spend long periods in hospital. In the last years of his life, he did no mathematics. Instead, he became obsessed with the idea that William Shakespeare's plays were written by Sir Frances Bacon. He wrote about his theories at length. Sadly, he died in Halle Sanatorium in 1918. His mathematical legacy lives on.

ALBERT EINSTEIN
1879-1955, GERMANY

$E=mc^2$ $E=mc^2$

Albert Einstein did not begin to talk until he was four, making his grandmother think he was not very bright. Einstein wasn't interested in school. He remembered later that one of his teachers had told him he would never amount to anything. However, he soon showed that he had a gift for mathematics and science—and thinking creatively!

When Einstein was five, his father bought him a compass. He was fascinated by the invisible force of magnetism that made the needle move.

When Einstein was 15, his family moved to Milan. Einstein was left in Munich to study, but he soon ran away to join his family. At 16, he applied to the Polytechnic Academy in Zürich. He was told he could attend only if he completed his schooling, which he did. His mathematics scores were exceptional but he became known for being disorganized and forgetting appointments.

In 1900, Einstein graduated with a degree in mathematics and physics. Unable to get a job teaching, Einstein started work tutoring children. In 1903, he got a job at the **patents** office in Bern. When he came home from work, he developed his own theories about matter, gravity, space, time, and light.

Einstein discovered new ways to work out the size of **molecules** and how particles move. In 1905, he published four papers which altered the course of modern physics. Perhaps the most important of these was his Theory of Relativity, which explains how gravity bends space. He also developed his famous equation $e = mc^2$. This means that energy (e) equals mass (m) times the speed of light, squared (c^2). It shows that mass can be turned into energy and vice versa. This theory later helped to explain the energy source of the Sun and other stars.

Einstein's work was interrupted by World War I (1914–1918). He was a pacifist, which means that he opposed war. In 1921, he was awarded the Nobel Prize in Physics and went around the world giving lectures. When the Nazi Party rose to power in Germany, Einstein was criticized because he was Jewish. Jewish people became increasingly at risk in Germany, so Einstein moved to the USA in 1933. He lectured at Princeton University. In the late 1930s, scientists began to work on the idea that $e = mc^2$ might make a **nuclear bomb** possible. After nuclear bombs were dropped on Japan at the end of World War II, Einstein formed the Emergency Committee of Atomic Scientists, working to control the spread of nuclear technology. In 1955, Einstein died aged 76, having continued to work on discoveries about heat, gravity, and relativity. His work had changed the course of physics and mathematics forever.

MARY CARTWRIGHT
1900-1998, UK

Dame Mary Lucy Cartwright was a British mathematician who was destined to do great things! When Cartwright went to university in 1919, she was one of only five women at Oxford University studying mathematics. Thankfully, times have changed.

Cartwright graduated with a first class degree in 1923. She worked as a teacher and then returned to Oxford to study for her doctorate, a higher qualification.

Cartwright was the first woman mathematician to be elected to the Royal Society, the UK's national academy of sciences. She also became Mistress of Girton College in Cambridge.

She was a pioneer of chaos theory. This is a mathematical theory that says a small difference at the start of a process can create major changes as time goes on. This is why weather is so hard to predict over a course of days—even for supercomputers. A small change in conditions can make a massive change in the predicted pattern of weather.

During World War II, Cartwright worked with the British Department of Scientific and Industrial Research. She helped to solve problems for radar scientists with her mathematical theories. Radar uses energy called radio waves, which bounce off objects, revealing their position.

She died aged 97, leaving behind books such as *The Mathematical Mind*. She also left a legacy for women—the knowledge that they too could be brilliant mathematicians.

ALAN TURING
1912-1954, UK

Alan Turing was a brilliant mathematician. His skills broke codes that shortened World War II and he designed one of the first stored program computers, the Automatic Computing Engine.

During World War II, Turing worked for the Government Code and Cypher School at Bletchley Park, England. He worked on breaking German codes used with the Enigma Machine. This machine sent messages in code so that they stayed secret and could not be read easily by the enemy. Estimates say his work shortened the war by up to two years and saved 14 million lives.

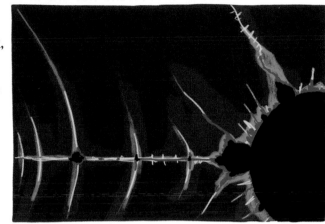

After the war, Turing's work continued. He worked at the National Physical Laboratory and designed the Automatic Computing Engine. In 1948, he joined the Computing Machine Laboratory at Manchester University. Turing's work made him one of the founders of the development of artificial intelligence (AI). He developed the Turing Test, a way to work out whether or not a computer program can think like a human being.

This talented man's life was ruined in 1952 when he was prosecuted for having a relationship with another man, which was illegal in the UK until 1967. Sadly, Alan Turing took his own life in 1954, 16 days before his 42nd birthday. In 2009, the British Prime Minister Gordon Brown made an official apology for the way Turing had been treated. In 2013, Queen Elizabeth II issued a pardon.

Today, the Turing Trust marks the amazing contribution Turing made to mathematics and computing. The Trust works to bring computers to communities that do not have them, keeping Turing's legacy alive.

Years after his death, Alan Turing is still being remembered. Benedict Cumberbatch played Alan Turing in the 2014 film *The Imitation Game*. Today, a building that houses the mathematics department at Manchester University is named after him. There is a bronze statue of Turing in Sackville Gardens in Manchester. There is another statue, made from half a million pieces of Welsh slate, at Bletchley Park. It was created by Stephen Kettle. In 2021, a £50 note was issued by the Bank of England featuring Turing.

MARJORIE LEE BROWNE
1914-1979, USA

Marjorie Lee Browne was born in Tennessee in 1914. At that time, schools were segregated in the USA, so she went to a Black school called LeMoyne High School. She attended Howard University in Washington DC, graduating in 1935.

Browne moved to New Orleans, where she worked as a teacher. After a year, she became restless and moved to Ann Arbor to attend the University of Michigan. She earned a master's degree in 1939 and a doctorate in 1949. She was only the third African-American woman to earn a PhD.

Later that year, Browne began teaching at North Carolina College, where she stayed for 30 years. For the first 25 years she was the only person in the mathematics department with a PhD in mathematics.

In 1960, Browne set up a computer center with a grant she obtained from IBM for $60,000. This was an amazing achievement: It was one of the first computers in an academic setting and the first at a historically African-American school.

Over the course of her life, Browne received many awards. She was part of the Women's Research Society and the Mathematical Association of America. She was one of the first African-American women to be part of the advisory council to the National Science Foundation. Throughout her career, she worked to support and help gifted mathematics students, even helping them financially.

KATHERINE JOHNSON
1918-2020, USA

Born Katherine Coleman in Virginia in 1918, Katherine was sent away to school with her brothers and sisters. This was necessary because there were no local schools beyond sixth grade for African-American students at that time. Schools were segregated, which means white children went to one school and Black children went to another.

She was very bright, and was only 14 when she went to West Virginia State College to study mathematics. She graduated in 1937 then spent two years teaching. She was picked to attend West Virginia University in 1939, becoming one of the first African-American students to attend. However, she left to get married and spent the next 13 years raising her family. In the 1940s, most women were expected to stay home to look after children rather than work outside the home. When her children were a little older, Johnson went back to teaching in schools.

In 1952, Johnson started working at Langley Aeronautical Laboratory. She worked in an all-African-American, all-woman computing unit. She worked on Project Mercury, the USA's first human spaceflight program. In 1969, her calculations helped the Apollo 11 mission, which put the first humans on the Moon.

OUT OF CURIOSITY

The book *Hidden Figures*, which was made into a movie, made Katherine Johnson famous around the world. When she was asked about her pioneering work as an African-American woman in the world of mathematics and space research, she said, "I was only doing my job."

JOHN HORTON CONWAY
1937-2020, UK

By the age of 11, John Conway knew he wanted to be a mathematician. He was a shy teenager, but tried to be more outgoing when he went to Cambridge University to study mathematics. He became an avid gamer. He would eventually be known as "the world's most charismatic mathematician," so it must have worked!

Sir Michael Atiyah, the former president of the Royal Society, described Conway as "the most magical mathematician in the world."

Conway graduated in 1959 and started to research number theory. In 1964, he was awarded his PhD and lectured at Cambridge University. He made many contributions to the world of mathematics and coding. His first experiments were done with a pen and paper but now there are hundreds of computer programs that use his system.

Conway became a fellow of the Royal Society "for Improving Natural Knowledge" in 1981. In 1986, Conway moved to the USA to lecture at Princeton University. He was very generous with his time and spent many summers teaching at mathematics camps for children and teenagers.

Conway invented lots of unusual algorithms, such as the best way to read through a pile of double-sided papers. He loved to teach and carried all sorts of items such as decks of cards, dice, ropes, and even a toy Slinky, to help him explain ideas in a fun way.

Tragically, he died of complications from COVID-19 in April 2020.

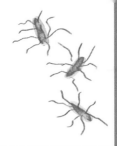

FERN YVETTE HUNT
(1948-PRESENT), USA

Fern Hunt is an American mathematician known for her work in applied mathematics (where mathematics is used in different fields, such as biology, medicine, and business). She has also done research in biomathematics, looking at patterns in tiny living things called bacteria.

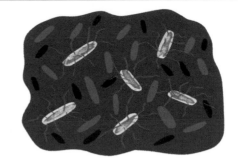

Hunt was born in 1948 in New York. She was a bright child and got a chemistry set for Christmas when she was aged nine. This sparked her interest in science, so her teacher encouraged her to do more. She attended Bryn Mawr College and graduated in 1969. She went on to earn a masters and PhD in mathematics from the Courant Institute of Mathematics at New York University.

Hunt lectured at the University of Utah and then moved to Howard University in Washington DC, carrying on with her research at the same time. Throughout her career, Hunt has lectured at colleges and universities to encourage students to become mathematicians. She uses her experiences as an African-American woman in mathematics to inspire others.

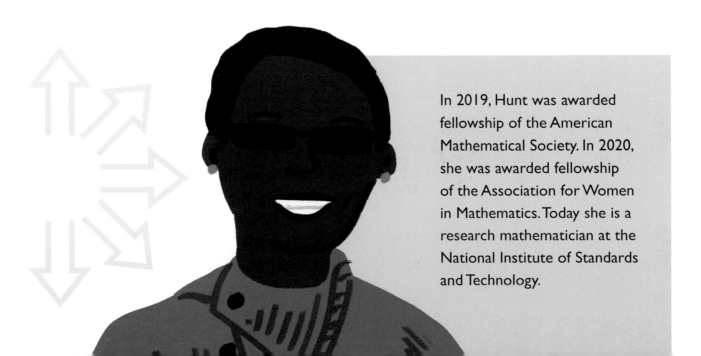

In 2019, Hunt was awarded fellowship of the American Mathematical Society. In 2020, she was awarded fellowship of the Association for Women in Mathematics. Today she is a research mathematician at the National Institute of Standards and Technology.

MARYAM MIRZAKHANI
1977-2017, IRAN

Iranian mathematician Maryam Mirzakhani was an expert in complex geometry. She used huge canvases on the floor to sketch out her ideas. Her area of mathematics is so complex it has been called "science-fiction mathematics." She solved things seen as unsolvable, and rewrote the mathematical understanding of spheres, donuts, and curved 3D shapes.

As a teenager, Mirzakhani won gold medals in the 1994 and 1995 International Mathematical Olympiads for high-school students. She attended the Sharif University of Technology in Tehran, graduating with a BSc in mathematics in 1999. She moved to the US and studied for a PhD at Harvard. From 2004 to 2008, she lectured at Princeton and in 2008 she became a professor at Stanford. Over the course of her career, she won many awards. In 2005 she was named in *Popular Science* magazine's Brilliant 10 as one of the top young minds in the world.

In 2014, Mirzakhani became the first woman to win the Fields Medal, mathematics' highest award. Tragically, this amazing mind was lost to the world when she died in 2017 aged 40, from breast cancer. The International Council for Science has declared May 12, Maryam Mirzakhani's birthday, as International Women in Mathematics Day. In 2020, on International Day of Women and Girls in STEM, Mirzakhani was named as one of seven female scientists who shaped the world.

TERENCE TAO
(1975-PRESENT), AUSTRALIA

Terry Tao was a child prodigy. At age eight, he achieved a SAT score of 760 out of 800 in a college-admission mathematics test. When he was nine, Tao began to study mathematics at Flinders University. He won a gold medal at the International Mathematical Olympiad in 1988, at the age of 12.

When Tao was 16, he graduated with a science degree from Flinders University. He earned his master's degree when he was 17. In 1992, he won a Fulbright Scholarship to carry out research at Princeton University in the USA. By the age of 21, he had earned his PhD. In 1996, he began lecturing at the University of California (UCLA). When he was 24, he became a full professor, the youngest person to ever achieve that status. In 2006, he was awarded the Fields Medal for excellence in mathematics, and in 2014, the Breakthrough Prize in Mathematics.

Tao's research in applied mathematics has led to faster magnetic resonance imaging (MRI) scans, which can save lives. His calculations have also been used in the search for other galaxies. He is one of the most respected mathematicians in the world.

GLOSSARY

algebra: To use unknown quantities (often given letters) with numbers to create formulas.

algorithm: A way of setting out a mathematical procedure to find an answer.

arc: A section of the circumference of a circle.

area: The size that a surface takes up. It can be measured in in^2 or cm^2.

arithmetic: Helps us work out addition, subtraction, division, and multiplication calculations.

artificial intelligence: A computer program that is able to think and learn.

axis, axes: A real or imaginary reference line. Graphs have horizontal and vertical axes. An axis in reflectional symmetry divides an object in half.

chord: A straight line that joins two points on the circumference of a circle.

circuit board: Holds connecting electronic components together.

circumference: A measure of the distance all the way around the edge, or perimeter, of a circle.

computer chip: A small piece of silicon that holds electronic parts. Computer chips allow a computer to carry out operations and to interpret and execute instructions.

cuboid: 3D shape. Most boxes are cuboids. Cuboids have six rectangular faces, and all of their angles are right angles.

diameter: The diameter of a circle is the distance running across a circle through the center, from edge to edge.

ellipse: 2D shape that looks like a flattened circle.

encrypt: If something is encrypted it is made hard to read and decipher

equation: A mathematical statement that contains an "equals" sign. The sign shows that two expressions are equal.

factor: A whole number that divides exactly into another number. A factor multiplies with another number to make a third number.

Fibonacci sequence: A series of numbers. The next number in the sequence is found by adding the two numbers before it.

finite: Means possible to be counted; has an end.

force: A push or pull, that can make things move, change direction or speed, or change shape.

fossil fuels: Fuels such as oil, coal, and gas, naturally created by the compression of the remains of prehistoric plant life and animals.

fractals: Patterns that repeat at different scales. They are not random, but are a single geometric pattern repeated at different magnifications.

frequencies: Electromagnetic waves (such as radio waves) are classified according to their frequencies.

functions: A function has an input, a rule, and an output. The output is always related to the input. A simple function might be "multiply by three." If the input is two, the output in this case would be six.

geometry: The study of shapes and their properties (such as faces, vertices, and edges).

golden ratio: A special number just about equal to 1.618. The ratio of 1.618 to 1 is said to create a beautiful shape.

graph: A diagram used to represent information in a visual form.

gravity: The force that pulls objects toward each other.

laser: An instrument that can produce a powerful and narrow beam of light. A laser is sometimes used for measuring, cutting materials, or medical operations.

leap year: A leap year has 366 days and happens every four years. The Earth's orbit of the Sun takes 365.256 days, so we make up the time we lose each year (when we say the year lasts 365 days) by adding a day to each fourth year—February 29.

length: How long something is or the distance from one end of something to the other end.

lunar: Means "to do with the Moon."

mass: The quantity of matter in an object.

microchip: A small piece of silicon that holds electronic parts. They are used in computers and other electronic devices.

molecule: The smallest unit of a substance that has all the properties of that substance.

number theory: Explains what some types of numbers are and what properties they have.

observatory: A place for studying natural objects and events both on Earth and in space. Astronomical observatories only observe space.

operations: Mathematical processes for working things out.

orbit: The path an object takes when it goes around a planet, star, or moon.

parallel: If lines are parallel, they are the same distance apart and do not touch.

patent: A legal document that gives an inventor the right to stop other people making their invention.

pi: A term used by mathematicians to describe a value which is the circumference of a circle divided by its diameter.

polygons: 2D shapes made up of straight lines, angles, and points.

polyhedron: 3D shape with flat faces and flat edges.

precipitation: Water falling as rain, sleet, snow, and hail.

probability: The chance that something will occur.

prodigy: Someone under the age of 10 who is able to do amazing things at an adult level in terms of music, science, mathematics, and other academic and artistic areas.

product: The result when two numbers are multiplied.

program (computer): A set of instructions that can be carried out by a computer to perform a task or set of tasks.

prototype: A simple model that helps inventors test out ideas.

quadrilateral: A type of polygon with four sides and four angles.

radius: The radius of a circle is the distance between the center of the circle and the edge or perimeter of the circle.

ratio: The comparison of two values of the same kind.

reflectional symmetry: If a shape or an object can be divided in half by a line, and the two halves match exactly, the shape or object has reflectional (or mirror) symmetry.

renewable energy: Energy that is limitless and can be generated from infinitely available sources such as wind and water power.

rotational symmetry: A shape has rotational symmetry if, when it is turned around its central point, it matches its original outline one or more times.

scale (map): The scale on a map tells us the ratio of a distance on the map to a distance on the ground.

seismic waves: The shock waves from an earthquake that travel through the ground.

servers: A computer or system that provides data and programs to other computers.

simulation (computer): A way to see things happen without them actually taking place. It can be used to predict the way things might happen.

software (computers): The operating system and programs on a computer.

solar: Means "to do with the Sun."

supercomputer: A computer with huge memory that performs at high speeds.

surface water (in terms of weather prediction): Water that is found gathered together such as oceans and lakes.

symmetry: Symmetry in an object or shape means either side of the line of symmetry is a mirror image of the other half. There may be one or many lines of symmetry (see also: rotational symmetry and reflectional symmetry.)

temperature: How hot or cold something is.

terrain: Landforms such as mountains.

tessellation: A pattern of 2D shapes that fit together with no gaps.

triangulate (earthquake): When scientists are looking for the epicenter of an earthquake they map out when the waves reach three fixed points. The central point is the epicenter.

trigonometry: The study of the relationships between the angles and sides of triangles.

vertices: The points in shapes where edges meet.

volume: The space occupied by an object.

weight: How heavy something is.

INDEX